I0129803

Rule Making in North Carolina

Richard B. Whisnant

UNC SCHOOL OF GOVERNMENT

THE UNIVERSITY of NORTH CAROLINA at CHAPEL HILL

School of Government, UNC Chapel Hill

ESTABLISHED IN 1931, the Institute of Government provides training, advisory, and research services to public officials and others interested in the operation of state and local government in North Carolina. The Institute and the university's Master of Public Administration Program are the core activities of the School of Government at The University of North Carolina at Chapel Hill.

Each year approximately 14,000 public officials and others attend one or more of the more than 200 classes, seminars, and conferences offered by the Institute. Faculty members annually publish up to fifty books, bulletins, and other reference works related to state and local government. Each day that the General Assembly is in session, the Institute's Daily Bulletin, available in print and electronic format, reports on the day's activities for members of the legislature and others who need to follow the course of legislation. An extensive Web site (www.sog.unc.edu) provides access to publications and faculty research, course listings, program and service information, and links to other useful sites related to government.

Operating support for the School of Government's programs and activities comes from many sources, including state appropriations, local government membership dues, private contributions, publication sales, course fees, and service contracts. For more information about the School, the Institute, and the MPA program, visit the Web site or call (919) 966-5381.

Michael R. Smith, DEAN
Thomas H. Thornburg, SENIOR ASSOCIATE DEAN
Patricia A. Langelier, ASSOCIATE DEAN FOR OPERATIONS
Ann Cary Simpson, ASSOCIATE DEAN FOR DEVELOPMENT AND COMMUNICATIONS
Bradley G. Volk, ASSOCIATE DEAN FOR FINANCE AND BUSINESS TECHNOLOGY

FACULTY

Gregory S. Allison	Robert L. Farb	John Rubin
Stephen Allred (on leave)	Joseph S. Ferrell	John L. Saxon
David N. Ammons	Milton S. Heath Jr.	Jessica Smith
A. Fleming Bell, II	Cheryl Daniels Howell	Carl Stenberg
Maureen M. Berner	Joseph E. Hunt	John B. Stephens
Frayda S. Bluestein	Willow Jacobson	Charles A. Szypszak
Mark F. Botts	Robert P. Joyce	Vaughn Upshaw
Joan G. Brannon	Diane Juffras	A. John Vogt
Mary Maureen Brown	David M. Lawrence	Bradley G. Volk
Anita R. Brown-Graham	Janet Mason	Gary A. Wagner
William A. Campbell	Laurie L. Mesibov	Aimee Wall
Anne M. Dellinger	Jill D. Moore	W. Mark C. Weidemaier
Shea Riggsbee Denning	Jonathan Q. Morgan	Richard B. Whisnant
James C. Drennan	David W. Owens	Gordon P. Whitaker
Richard D. Ducker	William C. Rivenbark	

© 2005
School of Government
The University of North Carolina at Chapel Hill

Printed in the United States of America

21 20 19 18 17   2 3 4 5 6

ISBN 1-56011-443-7

ABOUT THE COVER

The painting on the cover, *Mobile Sector*, is by American artist
Caroleigh Robinson. Robinson received her B.F.A. from the Maryland
Institute College of Art in 1982 and her M.F.A. from the University of
North Carolina at Chapel Hill in 1984.

She has received numerous awards and has shown her work at a
variety of national and international venues. The cover painting was
exhibited in 1995 at the 58th Midyear National Painting Exhibition at
the Butler Institute of American Art in Youngstown, Ohio.

For more information about Robinson's work—in mixed media on
paper, painting, sculpture, installations, photography, and video—visit
her website at http://caroleigh_robinson.tripod.com/caroleighrobinson/.

Arbitrary Government is where a people have men set over them, without their choice or allowance; who have power to govern them, and judge their causes without a rule.

—**John Winthrop**, "Arbitrary Government
Described and the Government of the
Massachusetts Vindicated from that
Aspersion" (Boston, 1644)

Contents

Preface

This book has two aims. The first is to give practical advice on the way administrative rules are made in North Carolina. In giving practical advice and a description of current rule-making processes, this book is intended to fulfill the legislature's mandate in Section 150B-21.23 of the North Carolina General Statutes for "a manual that sets out the form and method for publishing a notice of rule-making proceedings and a notice of text in the North Carolina Register and for filing a rule in the North Carolina Administrative Code."

The second aim is to help build a factual understanding of the rule-making process and its historical evolution, so that scholars, critics, reformers, and those who directly participate in rule making will have a basis for erecting their own theories of ways to improve government action. This aim requires going beyond a description of how things currently work to some consideration of the history, theory, and political forces that shape the way rules are now made.

There is no doubt that rule making in North Carolina, as in other states and at the federal level, is a very powerful determinant of the effectiveness, efficiency, and fairness of government action. State rules limit and shape behavior in nearly every field of human endeavor. Unfortunately, it is difficult (and accordingly rare) for anyone who comes in contact with administrative rule making in the context of a particular rule to step back and consider the entire sweep of the rule-making process. Most people concerned with the system of rule making, including many of the administrators and legislators who oversee the process, cannot see the rule-making forest because of their focus on the one or two trees that most concern them.

To restate this book's aim, then: It is to explain how the individual trees grew, but also to give some sense of the rule-making forest and its evolving relationship to the other processes in government that make it so important. These include legislation and the various administrative regulatory mechanisms that exist other than rule making: adjudication, permitting and licensing, enforcement, and direct provision of information, goods, and services.

A handful of people do, at the time of this text, see the whole rule-making forest, and several of these people have been particularly helpful to the production of this book. They include Julian Mann, chief administrative law judge and the codifier of rules; Molly Masich, whose experience and role at the Office of Administrative Hearings makes her the foremost guide through the woods; Ruby Creech, whose able assistance ensures that the official publications work on a timely basis; Joseph DeLuca and Bobby Bryan at the Rules Review Commission, who face each month the unenviable task of reading all the proposed rules to make calls on their clarity, authority, and procedural correctness; Mary Shuping and Karen Cochrane-Brown in the General Assembly staff, who have helped the Joint Legislative Administrative Procedures Oversight Committee carry out its oversight function; Juanita Gaskill, Kris Horton, and Paul Wilms, each of whom generously offered their time and particular perspectives on the process to help make this book a reality; and the members of the North Carolina Bar Association's Administrative Law Section, particularly Curtis Venable, who has been an astute and constructive critic of the process for longer than he probably cares to remember. Needless to say, any errors or omissions in the text are the responsibility of the author and have occurred in spite of, not because of, the assistance of these dwellers in the rule-making forest.

Richard B. Whisnant

Chapel Hill
October 2005

Chapter 1

What is *rule making*?

Rule making is the process of making *rules*, and in the context of this book and of administrative law, these terms have very specific meanings. The context is important. The scope of this book and of the field is the making of rules by state administrative agencies. Agencies of state government have been given the power to limit what people can do, with state-sanctioned consequences, such as the loss of liberty or property, if these limits are not followed. Rules are the written form these limits take, and the text of a rule is the primary source that a court looks to when asked to enforce or to undo these limits. So rules are the legal underpinning of most other administrative regulatory actions, such as permitting and enforcement.

Rule making is the process that agencies must go through in order for their rules to be enforceable (unless they have some special exemption).[1] "A rule is not valid unless it is adopted in substantial compliance with [the Administrative Procedure Act, G.S. 150B, Article 2A]."[2]

This immediately establishes the importance of rules and rule making: rules, as this book discusses them, have the force of law. Thus another way to define rule making is "the process agencies use to make generally applicable law." Unless that process is in "substantial compliance" with the Administrative Procedure Act (APA), Chapter 150B, Article 2A of the North Carolina General Statutes (hereinafter G.S.), the administrative actions that emerge are not valid.

One important caveat to the above statement, a caveat that also applies to the scope of this book, is that a significant minority of North Carolina administrative agencies are wholly or partially exempted from the APA. Thus the following agencies are not subject to the rule-making requirements that this book covers. Note that as rule making has become more complex and costly, many other agencies have sought or desired exemptions, so one should check the very latest edition of the APA to make sure a given agency is covered. Between the first draft and the final manuscript for this book, five agencies were at least partially exempted and two exemptions were repealed, giving some indication of how unstable the APA coverage was in this period. As of the publication date of this book, the list of exempted agencies included

- The North Carolina National Guard in exercising its court-martial jurisdiction
- The Department of Human Resources in exercising its authority over the Camp Butner reservation granted in Article 6 of Chapter 122C of the General Statutes
- The Utilities Commission
- The Industrial Commission
- The Employment Security Commission
- The State Board of Elections in administering the complaint procedures of the Help America Vote Act of 2002[3]
- The Rules Review Commission
- The Department of Revenue, with respect to the notice and hearing requirements contained in Part 2 of Article 2A of Chapter 150B
- The North Carolina Global TransPark Authority with respect to the acquisition, construction, operation, or use, including fees or charges, of any portion of a cargo airport complex
- The Department of Correction, with respect to matters relating solely to persons in its custody or under its supervision, including prisoners, probationers, and parolees
- The North Carolina Teachers' and State Employees' Comprehensive Major Medical Plan in administering the Provisions of Parts 2 and 3 of Article 3 of Chapter 135 of the General Statutes
- The North Carolina Hazardous Waste Management Commission in administering the provisions of G.S. 130B-13 and G.S. 130B-14
- The North Carolina Federal Tax Reform Allocation Committee, with respect to the adoption of the annual qualified allocation plan required by 26 U.S.C. § 42(m) and any agency designated by the committee to the extent necessary to administer the annual qualified allocation plan
- The Department of Health and Human Services in adopting new or amending existing medical coverage policies under the state Medicaid program
- The Economic Investment Committee in developing criteria for

the Job Development Investment Grant Program under Part 2F of
Article 10 of Chapter 143B of the General Statutes
- The North Carolina State Ports Authority with respect to fees
established pursuant to G.S. 143B-454(a)(11)[4]
- The University of North Carolina[5]
- Units of local government[6]

Finally, in considering whether a given agency action is or is not
subject to the rule-making process, one must check the particular
statutory authorization for the agency's action (sometimes called the
"organic statutes"). An unfortunately significant trend in legislation
following the 1995 amendments to the North Carolina APA is for
agencies that are generally covered by the APA to be given some
particular exemption or special process for things the legislature would
like to see done quickly. This, along with the outright exemptions noted
above, further undermine one of the most basic policy goals of the APA
in regard to rule making, which is to establish a uniform process that
can be understood and predicted by everyone concerned with a rule.[7]
There has always been a ·tension within administrative law between
proponents of consistency and those who believe that administrative
processes are so inherently different that it is folly to try to fit them all
under one procedural scheme.[8]

What is a *rule*?

The exact meaning of *rule* in the North Carolina administrative law
context is found at G.S. 150B-2(8a). This section of the APA has definitions
that apply throughout the APA, and the definition of rule is far and
away the longest and most complicated of the definitions. This suggests
its importance. The form of the definition is a broad opening clause
that includes most pronouncements by agencies, followed by a series
of narrow exceptions that carve out certain agency activities and thus
exempt these narrow activities from having to go through the rule-
making process.

The basic definition

The broadly inclusive part of the definition is:

> "Rule" means any agency regulation, standard, or statement of
> general applicability that implements or interprets an enactment
> of the General Assembly or Congress or a regulation adopted
> by a federal agency or that describes the procedure or practice
> requirements of an agency. The term includes the establishment of a
> fee and the amendment or repeal of a prior rule.[9]

The first sentence very nearly covers any pronouncement by an agency that could have the force of law. The second sentence notes two important types of agency action that might arguably not be within the coverage of the first sentence, but that are expressly included as rules.

The importance of the last clause, the "amendment or repeal of a prior rule," is that whether an agency is making an entirely new rule, is revising an existing rule, or is even repealing a rule, the basic rule-making process is the same.[10] This has implications for the ease with which rules can be changed or repealed once they are deemed to be in need of revision. As the rule-making process has grown increasingly complicated, time-consuming, and costly, there has also been a certain degree of "lock in" of old rules. The rule-making process in North Carolina, in other words, has not evolved to allow flexible, incremental changes in rules. Any change, with certain narrow exceptions to be discussed, must work through the same process as an entirely new rule.

In the definition of "rule," following this broad opening paragraph, there are no less than eleven categories of agency pronouncements that are excluded from coverage as "rules," and thus excluded from having to go through the rule-making process to be established or changed.[11] The eleven categories are

a. Statements concerning only the internal management of an agency or group of agencies within the same principal office or department enumerated in G.S. 143A-11 or 143B-6, including policies and procedures manuals, if the statement does not directly or substantially affect the procedural or substantive rights or duties of a person not employed by the agency or group of agencies.

b. Budgets and budget policies and procedures issued by the Director of the Budget, by the head of a department, as defined by G.S. 143A-2 or G.S. 143B-3, by an occupational licensing board, as defined by G.S. 93B-1, or by the State Board of Elections.

c. Nonbinding interpretative statements within the delegated authority of an agency that merely define, interpret, or explain the meaning of a statute or rule.

d. A form, the contents or substantive requirements of which are prescribed by rule or statute.

e. Statements of agency policy made in the context of another proceeding, including
    1. Declaratory rulings under G.S. 150B-4.
    2. Orders establishing or fixing rates or tariffs.

f. Requirements, communicated to the public by the use of signs or symbols, concerning the use of public roads, bridges, ferries, buildings, or facilities.

g. Statements that set forth criteria or guidelines to be used by the staff of an agency in performing audits, investigations, or inspections; in settling financial disputes or negotiating financial arrangements; or in the defense, prosecution, or settlement of cases.

h.   Scientific, architectural, or engineering standards forms, or procedures, including design criteria and construction standards used to construct or maintain highways, bridges, or ferries.

i.   Job classification standards, job qualifications, and salaries established for positions under the jurisdiction of the State Personnel Commission.

j.   Establishment of the interest rate that applies to tax assessments under G.S. 105-241.1 and the variable component of the excise tax on motor fuel under G.S. 105-434.

k.   The State Medical Facilities Plan, if the Plan has been prepared with public notice and hearing as provided in G.S. 131E-176(25), reviewed by the Commission for compliance with G.S. 131E-176(25), and approved by the Governor.[12]

Most of these exceptions are fairly clear and narrow and have presented little problem in application. Others, notably the exceptions for "internal statements" and "interpretive rules," have presented thorny issues for a long time, at both state and federal levels. Further discussion is given to them below.

The first exception to the broad, general definition of rule covers

The internal management exception

> [s]tatements concerning only the internal management of an agency or group of agencies within the same principal office or department enumerated in G.S. 143A-11 or 143B-6, including policies and procedures manuals, if the statement does not directly or substantially affect the procedural or substantive rights or duties of a person not employed by the agency or group of agencies.[13]

As with most legal definitions, the cases that are clearly "in" or "out" of this definition are fairly easy to grasp. Most administrative agencies have policies or procedures for their employees to use covering things such as going to work in bad weather, use of state vehicles, dress, office equipment, media relations, and so forth. Some of these policies, such as the examples given above, are likely to have only minor or indirect effects on persons outside the agency. Others, such as departmental policies on public records, are likely to have a direct, potentially significant, effect on persons outside the agency. In the former case, the exception to the broad, general definition of rule excludes the policies and allows agencies to create valid statements concerning *internal management* without going through the rule-making process. These are most likely to be of legal interest in the context of personnel proceedings. In the latter case, agencies may have policies (such as for public records) that have not gone through the rule-making process, but those policies have no legal force. If they are challenged, a court should not uphold them.

There are two main sources of difficulty with this exception. One is knowing where the line is crossed to a "direct or substantial effect" on the rights or duties of persons outside the agency. The other is in deciding who are "persons employed by the agency or group of agencies."

As to the first type of difficult case, there is little law to go on in drawing the line. One principle underlying the APA suggests that courts should be wary of agencies that raise this exception as a defense. That principle is the principle of fair notice and ability to comment, which principle is embedded both in the procedures for adopting rules and in the overall policy of the APA to separate out the functions of "rule making, investigation, advocacy, and adjudication."[14] In the case of internal agency statements, it is rarely the case that affected persons outside the agency are given notice and an opportunity to comment before the statement begins to shape agency practice. Notice and an opportunity to comment are two of the foundations on which the legitimacy of agency rules are built.

As to the second type of difficult case, concerning who is or is not a "person employed by the agency or group of agencies," the problems arise primarily out of the novel forms of government that emerged with increasing frequency in the late twentieth century. Public–private partnerships, nonprofit organizations that exist mainly to support government functions, and hybrid forms of state and local government units have proliferated, creating classes of agencies and agency personnel that are not always clearly "in" or "out" of a given department of state government. Here again, there will be easier and harder cases.[15]

The easy case is illustrated by a former practice of the Motor Fleet Management Division within the Department of Administration, which is responsible for the state motor fleet, of having policies and procedures governing the use of state vehicles by all state employees. These policies were originally not adopted as rules, but this practice seemed clearly invalid in light of the APA.[16] The state motor fleet policies and procedures do have a direct and substantial effect on the rights and duties of persons outside the Department of Administration. The test is not whether the affected persons are state employees, but rather whether they are in the same principal department as the agency making the policies.

Interpretive rules: Rules versus policies, procedures, and guidance documents

Interpretive rules are

> [n]onbinding interpretative statements within the delegated authority of an agency that merely define, interpret, or explain the meaning of a statute or rule.[17]

The interpretive rule exception has presented numerous interpretive problems at the state level and with its federal counterpart.[18] Professor

Charles Daye of the University of North Carolina Law School, in his important review of North Carolina's then-new Administrative Procedure Act,[19] cited Professor Arthur Bonfield of the University of Iowa College of Law, reporter for the model state administrative procedure act, in support of the proposition that "generally speaking, interpretive rules carry no sanction, and if a sanction is involved, it is seen as emanating from the statute."[20] This is a possible justification for their exclusion from rule-making procedures.

The 1981 Model State APA gives a gloss: a rule that (1) purports only to define the meaning of a statute or other provision of law or precedent and (2) was issued by an agency that did not possess delegated authority to bind the courts with its definition of that statute or other provision of law or precedent.[21] This is an odd gloss, since no agency can really bind courts to a definition of a statute. At the federal level, though, and in some other states, there have been explicit attempts by courts to describe the extent to which they would defer to long-standing agency interpretations of their governing statutes, and there has normally been a great deal of deference afforded to these interpretations.[22] North Carolina courts have been less clear in their position on this pivotal issue.[23] The basic idea of this APA exception is that agencies may have internal interpretations of statutes and of their own rules; indeed, agencies must have these interpretations in order to carry out their responsibilities consistently within the agency. These interpretations may have some persuasive power, but they have no legal power to limit the reading that persons outside the agency give to the statute or rule, unless the agency is willing to go through the rule-making process. Even if the agency goes through the rule-making process for a rule interpreting another rule or statute, North Carolina courts will not necessarily defer to the agency's legal interpretation.

Deference to agency interpretation of statutes in North Carolina

The law on the proper deference by courts to agency interpretations of their own rules, or to agency rules that interpret statutes, is somewhat confusing in North Carolina. Support can be found in the cases for almost any position one might advance. The most commonly cited general approach is summed up by three rules stated in a recent North Carolina Supreme Court case:

> When the issue on appeal is whether a state agency erred
> in interpreting a regulatory term, an appellate court may freely
> substitute its judgment for that of the agency and employ de novo
> review. [1] *See* Brooks v. McWhirter Grading Co., 303 N.C. 573,
> 580-81, 281 S.E.2d 24, 29 (1981). However, the interpretation of
> a regulation by an agency created to administer that regulation is
> traditionally accorded some deference by appellate courts. [2] *See*
> *id. at* 581, 281 S.E.2d at 29.

The Commission administers the North Carolina Administrative Code regulations at issue here. N.C.G.S. § 17E-4 (1997). These regulations provide that "[t]he Commission may revoke, suspend or deny the certification of a justice officer when the Commission finds that . . . the certified officer has committed or been convicted of: . . . a crime or unlawful act defined in 12 NCAC 10B . 0103(10)(b) as a Class B misdemeanor within the five-year period prior to the date of appointment." 12 NCAC 10B .0204(d)(2) (Nov. 1995) (emphasis added). They also explain that "'Convicted' or 'Conviction' means and includes, for purposes of this Chapter, the entry of: . . . a plea of no contest." 12 NCAC 10B .0103(2)(c) (Nov. 1995).

These regulations are unambiguous. When the language of regulations is clear and unambiguous, there is no room for judicial construction, and courts must give the regulations their plain meaning. [3] *See* Correll v. Division of Social Serv., 332 N.C. 141, 144, 418 S.E.2d 232, 235 (1992).[24]

Thus review of legal interpretations is de novo (rather than a review on the record created by the agency), but the court will give some degree of deference to an agency's construction of its own statute, and will not disturb that interpretation if it is clear and unambiguous.[25] One missing element in this analysis is the first step in recent federal cases construing the *Chevron* rule, namely, has the legislature expressed its intent on the issue unambiguously? If so, there is no gap for the agency interpretation to fill, and the court should follow the legislature's clear and unambiguous intention.[26]

Whatever the degree of deference accorded to agencies' promulgated rules that interpret statutes, the APA allows them to make nonbinding interpretations without going through the rule-making process.[27] Such nonbinding, nonpromulgated interpretive rules should be given no deference if challenged, of course, since the agency's avoidance of the rule-making process was premised on the theory that the interpretation had no legal effect outside the agency.

Summary:
What is a *rule*?

To sum up, the basic, inexact meaning of *rule* is a statement or standard of an executive branch agency that is meant to apply generally and that directly or substantially affects the rights or procedures of a person outside the agency.[28] But to answer precisely the question whether any given agency pronouncement is a rule and thus must be made through the rule-making process in order to be enforceable, one must work through the general paragraph and then the exceptions to the definition of rule in G.S. 150B-2(8a) and one must also research the underlying (organic) legislation that gave the agency authority to make the pronouncement in the first place. The organic legislation may exempt the agency pronouncement altogether or may alter the APA process.

The question sometimes arises as to the size of the unit implied by the term "rule." That is, when an agency proposes rule changes, it will often lump together several (often many) sections of the North Carolina Administrative Code (NCAC) and refer to them collectively as "the so-and-so rule." Is the rule then the entire collection of sections that have a common reason for being, or is the rule each individual section? The question is not a trivial one, since the APA rule-making provisions assign various rights and responsibilities based on each individual unit called a rule. For example, if the Rules Review Commission objects to a rule as lacking statutory authority, how much of an agency's regulations are put in doubt by the objection?

The answer in North Carolina, for most purposes, is that each separately numbered paragraph of the NCAC constitutes a rule. The numbers are four-digit numbers immediately following a decimal point; the numbers and letters before the decimal point represent a subchapter.[29] For example, rule 26 NCAC 2C.0201 is an individual rule stating the scope and importance of the codification approach in the North Carolina Administrative Code. The citation tells a reader this is chapter 26 of the NCAC (the chapter for all rules of the Office of Administrative Hearings), subchapter 2C (the subchapter for submission procedures for rules and other documents to be published in the North Carolina Register and the North Carolina Administrative Code), and rule .0201. This scope is not immediately clear from the definition of rule in the statutes, but it is the practice that has evolved in rule codification and it is supported by the statutory provisions on rule codification. For example, for each rule that is included in the NCAC, there must be a citation for the law under which the rule was adopted and a history note; this is presented by the codifier of rules on a section-by-section basis within the NCAC.[30] The codifier also has flexibility to alter the form of rules and to rearrange the order within rules, so on the question of the size of the unit represented by a rule, the codifier's approach is decisive.[31]

History note

Prior to adoption of Chapter 150B in 1985, when the APA was contained in G.S. Chapter 150A, what counted as a rule differed from the approach under Chapter 150B. Under the prior chapter, 150A, the term "rule" included matters subject to the formal rule-making process as well as other matters that were required to be filed with the attorney general's office, but not required to go through the notice and public comment procedure.[32] Accordingly, older cases (prior to 1985) on the definition and requirements of rule making must be read carefully to determine whether they would have been decided the same way under Chapter 150B.

What is the legal power of a rule?

As noted, rules (assuming they are properly made) have the force of law.[33] This means that a rule can be the basis for the state legally to deprive a person of liberty or property. This power is no different for administrative rules than for legislated law, or *statutes*. It also is no different, in its ultimate power, than the power of court-created law, or *common law*. Any or all of a rule, a statute, or common law can be the basis for legal action to deprive someone of property or liberty. Thus the fairness and legitimacy of the rule-making process are no less important than the fairness and legitimacy of the legislative and judicial processes, even though the latter two are much better known and more widely monitored. The stress here on fairness is underscored by two of the basic policy goals of the APA: first, uniformity, as noted above; second, the assurance that an agency is not acting arbitrarily when it affects the liberty and property interests of those outside the agency.[34]

One feature of rule making that gives some relief from this potential for lack of fairness and legitimacy is that agencies must be given the authority to make rules by the legislature, whereas the legislature itself and the courts get their authority to act directly through the constitution. Thus, to understand rule making, one must understand the scope and location of legislatively granted authority to make rules.

Who has authority to make rules?

Rule making, as discussed in this book, is a function of state agencies. There are many similarities, but also important differences, between the needs and capacities for state rule making as compared with rule making by federal agencies.[35] An *agency* is "an agency or an officer in the executive branch of the government of this State and includes the Council of State, the Governor's Office, a board, a commission, a department, a division, a council, and any other unit of government in the executive branch. A local unit of government is not an agency."[36] This is a variant of the broadly inclusive definition of agency proposed in the 1961 and 1981 Model State Administrative Procedures Acts, designed to make it clear that every executive branch agency of state government is covered, unless specifically exempted.[37] Specific jurisdiction, function, duration, or reporting relationships of the agency do not matter; if it is a state-created entity that carries out governmental work and is not a local government, a part of the legislature or a part of the judiciary, and it has no express exemption from the APA, it is governed by the APA.

Note that, unlike the 1981 Model State APA, the North Carolina APA has no express provision for the increasingly common governmental units that are hybrids between traditional state agencies and local governments.[38]

Examples are transit authorities, watershed authorities, and other groups that cut across county and municipal lines. Some agencies in this hybrid category, such as drainage districts and water and sewer conservation districts, have long been viewed in North Carolina as units of local government. Others have no such long history. Statewide jurisdiction should not be a prerequisite to coverage under the APA, and there is a gray area in the North Carolina statute for agencies that cover an area larger than a county but smaller than the state as a whole. The safest course for such agencies, in light of the inclusive nature of the APA, is to view themselves as covered and thus subject to the rule-making provisions whenever they wish to put policies in place that bind persons outside the agency.

The need for legislative authority

To make administrative rules an agency must have either an explicit grant of authority from the legislature or else its authority must be necessarily implied from other statutory duties created by the legislature.[39] Can authority be implied from the state constitution? This issue was raised, but not decided, in *State v. Whittle Communications.*[40] In general, administrative agencies have those powers expressly vested by statute and "those [implied] powers reasonably necessary for the agency to function properly. . . ."[41] Some examples of implied powers are the power to reserve a room and hold a meeting, the power to study a policy problem, and the power to confer with policy experts. These are powers that are generally taken for granted in the running of an agency that makes public policies through rule making. The legislature does not have to provide expressly for every single activity that an agency undertakes. On the other hand, the scope of "implied" powers should be viewed narrowly, since the authority to make rules must come expressly from a legislative (or constitutional) source. The implied powers are simply means to the end of carrying out the rule making that does have explicit authorization.

Other restrictions on what can be adopted as a rule

G.S. 150B-19 and other sources of law contain several additional restrictions on what can be adopted as a rule. An agency cannot adopt a rule that does one or more of the following:

- Enlarges professional and occupational licensing limits[42]
- Imposes liability for a criminal or civil penalty without express authority to do so[43]
- Merely repeats the language of a statute, another rule, or a federal regulation[44]
- Establishes fees without express authority to do so, other than fees for service to governmental units, copies of documents, transcripts of public hearings, courses and conferences, and data processing services[45]

- Allows waiver or modification of another rule, without specific guidelines in determining whether to waive or modify the requirement[46]
- Deprives citizens of constitutional rights—the federal and state constitutions being superior law to laws of the legislature as well as rules, an agency cannot override a constitutional right through rule making

The nondelegation doctrine and the need for guiding standards

The constitutions impose another type of restriction on what can be adopted as a rule. This is a restriction on the legislature's authority to delegate power to agencies. At some point, a delegation of rule-making authority, even though it is expressly made by the legislature, can become so broad that a court will strike it down as violating the *nondelegation doctrine*. This doctrine holds that the legislature, and only the legislature, has some ultimate reservoir of legislative power that cannot be delegated away. According to this doctrine, an agency cannot be handed what is, in essence, an open mandate to go and solve a policy problem without some degree of policy guidance from the legislature.

The exact nature of this inherently legislative power is very hard to determine. Agencies, in rule making, act as quasi legislatures, just as they act like quasi courts when they resolve particular applications and disputes. This is the genius of agencies, that they can combine these quasi-legislative and quasi-judicial functions and have them carried out by specially trained persons. But courts, in North Carolina as at the federal level, have occasionally read the constitution's directive that legislative, judicial, and executive branch powers should be separate and distinct to mean that some grants of rule-making authority to agencies might go too far or be too broad.

There has been an important evolution in the thinking of courts in North Carolina and elsewhere about the nondelegation doctrine over the past seventy years. Early cases, following the bar's concern about the rise of administrative power in the New Deal era, showed courts to be quite willing to strike down administrative action if not limited by legislated "adequate guiding standards."[47] Since its two much-maligned 1935 decisions, *Panama Refining Co. v. Ryan*,[48] and *A.L.A. Schechter Poultry Corp. v. United States*,[49] the U.S. Supreme Court has not struck administrative rules for violating the nondelegation doctrine.[50] A federal court of appeals revived the doctrine in 2001 in a case challenging the U.S. Environmental Protection Agency's air standards, but the Supreme Court reversed the court of appeals.[51] Later North Carolina cases still use the language of "adequate guiding standards," but their actual rulings have moved toward Professor Davis's theory that adequate procedures may suffice to support rule making, even in the absence of clearly articulated, definite, legislative standards.[52] In its two primary decisions on point, the North Carolina Supreme Court has said:

[t]he test is whether the delegation is accompanied by adequate guiding standards. If so, the delegation will be upheld. The need to delegate a limited portion of legislative powers in order to effectively utilize administrative expertise must be reconciled with the constitutional mandate that the legislature retain in its own hands the supreme legislative power. Jernigan v. State, 279 N.C. 556, 184 S.E.2d 259 (1971). We must insure that the decision-making by the administrative agency is not arbitrary and unreasoned and that the agency is not asked to make important policy choices that might just as easily be made by the legislature. Adams v. N.C. Department of Natural and Economic Resources, *supra*. The goals and policies set forth by the legislature for the agency to apply in exercising its powers need be only as specific as the circumstances permit. *Id.* N.C. Turnpike Authority v. Pine Island, Inc., 265 N.C. 109, 143 S.E.2d 319 (1965).[53]

One important corollary is that the test of adequacy is made with reference to the full range of statutory guidance that the legislature has given to an agency, not just the narrow standards included in a particular grant of rule-making authority.[54]

Another important corollary of these main nondelegation cases is that the procedures required for rule making under the APA are themselves cited by the Supreme Court as partial assurance that the nondelegation doctrine was not violated. This means that rule making outside the APA context could be held to need a higher degree of legislative guidance than does rule making within the APA context.

There are also delegation questions about rule making that arise within an agency. Two sorts of questions commonly arise. First, to which agency is the grant of rule-making authority given? Second, within that agency, how far and under what conditions can the authority to make rules be subdelegated?

The first of these questions most commonly arises because of North Carolina's frequent use of both permanently staffed departments, consisting of career state employees along with appointed agency heads, as well as commissions, consisting of appointed citizens who usually serve part-time and without pay. Both are types of "agency," and both can be given rule-making authority. Sometimes the grant of authority is ambiguous as to who gets the power. If the legislation says "the Secretary" or "the Department" shall have the power to make rules, or conversely "the Commission" shall have such power, and those terms are defined elsewhere in the statutory article or chapter into which the legislation is codified, there is little or no doubt who is the ultimate wielder of the rule-making power. But occasionally legislation will be written in passive voice or will otherwise be ambiguous about the locus of rule-making power.[55]

Some North Carolina cases give explicit recognition to the need for delegation as an efficient way of governing a complex society. This need suggests a functional test for delegation doctrine questions: Is there a regulatory task to be performed that cannot be effectively performed by the legislature without assistance of a delegate or without such a great expenditure of time as to lead to neglect of equally important business?[56]

On the second of these questions, concerning subdelegation, Professor Davis credits President Kennedy with inspiring courts to allow wider, more frequent use of subdelegation as a concession to the way governments now operate and to the types of matters with which senior agency officials need to be concerned:

> The reduction of existing delays in our regulatory agencies requires the elimination of needless work at their top levels. . . . [U]necessary and unimportant details occupy far too much of the time and energy of agency members, and prevent full and expeditious consideration of the more important issues.
>
> The remedy is a far wider range of delegations to smaller panels of agency members, or to agency employee boards, and to give their decisions and those of the hearing examiners a considerable degree of finality, conserving the full agency membership for issues of true moment. Such delegation would not be an abnegation of responsibility if the agency retained a discretionary right of review of all such decisions, exercisable either upon its own initiative or upon the petition of a party demonstrating to the agency that the matter in issue is of such substantial importance that it calls for determination at the highest agency level.[57]

What was an important issue in public administration for federal agencies in 1961 is now just as important for many state agencies: the reality is that senior agency officials often have neither the time nor expertise themselves to oversee the development of rules and rule changes. So subdelegation is a necessary fact of modern government in North Carolina. Subdelegation, meaning the transfer of rule-making authority from the head of an agency to a subordinate, should normally be allowed by reviewing courts, unless expressly prohibited by statute, so long as the subdelegation is within the agency and appears reasonably calculated to improve the quality of the resulting rules.[58] The "within agency" principle is important because the agency head retains the right and ability to review and change actions within the agency head's control. As a general proposition, courts do not allow agencies to delegate authority to private parties.[59]

Each principal state department in the governor's cabinet, as listed in G.S. 143B-6, is said by statute to have an agency head to be appointed by the governor and to serve at the pleasure of the governor.[60] Furthermore, the same Executive Organization Act of 1973, which set up this system of principal departments, also provided that "the head of each principal State department may assign or reassign any function vested in him or in his department to any subordinate officer or employee of his department."[61] Presumably, then, there is ample authority for a delegation from a department secretary to another person within the department. The Office of Administrative Hearings acknowledges this possibility (and the reality of conducting agency affairs efficiently) by requiring agencies to submit copies of their delegations to the Office of Administrative Hearings, in so far as they concern rule making. "If the agency head has designated its authority to another pursuant to G.S. 143B-10(a), then the agency shall submit a copy of such designation. It is only necessary to submit one copy of such designation with all rules filed by an agency for a single month's review by the commission."[62] All of this would seem to be capable of alteration by a given governor, at any time, given the constitutional provisions for the governor to organize the executive branch in whatever manner the governor believes best serves the constitutional responsibility to see that the laws are faithfully executed.[63]

How agencies make law: Rule making versus adjudication

APA rule making is not the only choice potentially open to an agency to make law. It is the only choice to create broadly applicable standards or requirements that are legally binding (unless the agency has an exemption from the rule-making process requirements). But through adjudication, that is, making decisions about the application of law and policy on a case-by-case basis, agencies can also create law, even though the courts will not necessarily give that law binding effect on persons who are not parties to the adjudication. Adjudication covers everything from permit decisions and informal resolution of disputes and questions to formal administrative adjudication that works much like lawsuits in court. In North Carolina, the formal adjudicatory process for persons who are aggrieved by agency decisions of agencies subject to the APA is normally the "contested case" process set out in articles 3 and 3A of G.S. 150B.

Sometimes agency action is hard to categorize as either rule making or adjudication. For example, in rate-making proceedings of the Commissioner of Insurance and the Utilities Commission, the agency decision maker makes a decision on the application of an individual regulated entity. But the decision has broadly applicable and legally binding consequences. In 1980, the North Carolina Supreme Court considered the question whether the Commissioner of Insurance had the choice of proceeding by rule making or by adjudication in setting rates. While the case was decided under a predecessor statute to the APA, its discussion still explains much of what motivates the provisions of the current APA: to assure fairness and the absence of arbitrary government.

> The rule-making power of an administrative agency is restricted by law apart from the statute conferring power and an agency having authority to effectuate the policies of a particular statute may not effectuate such policies so singlemindedly that it wholly ignores other and equally important legislative objectives. . . . This is especially true in the case of agencies which have both accusatorial and judgmental powers. The potential for unfairness and abuse is obvious in a situation in which an administrative officer is vested with broad rule-making powers, determining the admissibility and weight of evidence in hearings and making the final determination on the merits of an action, as is the Commissioner of Insurance in ratemaking cases. Indeed, one of the fundamental purposes in the creation of administrative procedure acts was to minimize the potential of unfairness in embodying in one person or agency these various functions. *See generally* 1 Am. Jur. 2d, *Administrative Law* 78. Since an administrative agency is vested with powers both quasi-judicial and quasi-legislative, such procedural safeguards are essential.[64]

Critics and reformers of rule making in the 1990s and beyond often equated "rule making" with "regulation" and disparaged it accordingly. Thus rules and rule making have, in the minds of many, come to be seen as synonymous with onerous, inefficient, intrusive government action. This was the sentiment behind North Carolina's 1995 APA reforms. This criticism usually fails to consider the costs and benefits of alternative ways to regulate, primarily adjudication. Done properly, rule making is more efficient, fairer (at least in terms of consistency), and less arbitrary than making decisions entirely on a case-by-case basis.

Who collects and publishes the official version of the rules?

Rule making was originally conceived as a more flexible way to make law than by passing legislation or trying multiple lawsuits; thus rules were conceived as things that might change more frequently than statutes or the common law. The continued existence of this greater flexibility is questionable, at least, under North Carolina's current APA provisions for rule making. But whether or not rule making has accordingly lost its intended usefulness as a dynamic legal institution, rules still do change. It is thus important (and sometimes challenging) to know where and how to find the most current and official version of the rules.

The codifier of rules, who is by statute the chief administrative law judge of the Office of Administrative Hearings or a designated representative of the chief administrative law judge,[65] is the person responsible for keeping, codifying, and publishing the official version of the rules.[66] This official version is called the North Carolina Administrative Code (NCAC). Part 4 of Article 2A of G.S. 150B sets out the statutory requirements for publication of the NCAC. Once a rule is included in the NCAC, official or judicial notice can be taken of the rule, "and shall be taken when appropriate."[67]

All rules, notices of rule-making proceedings, and the text of proposed rules—as well as several other important categories of public information—must be published by the codifier of rules in a publication called the *North Carolina Register.*[68] The *North Carolina Register* must be published at least twice a month,[69] and there are statutory requirements governing the form in which rules and proposed rules are published.[70]

For agencies that are not subject to the APA but that nevertheless have "rules" that may be important in litigation, some steps must be taken to establish official versions of rules and the method of proving when and how rules were promulgated.[71] The statutes have particular requirements for rules of the North Carolina State Bar, the Building Code Council, the North Carolina Utilities Commission, and other agencies exempt from the APA rule-making proceedings.[72] The State Bar and exempt agencies other than the Utilities Commission must submit their rules for inclusion in the NCAC within thirty days after adoption of the rule.[73] The Utilities Commission publishes its rules separately, but still must submit its rules to the codifier of rules.[74]

Notes

1. The law actually says that would-be rules that are not properly created through the rule-making process are not "valid," not that they are not "enforceable." However, lack of enforceability is an important legal outcome of a law or rule that is "invalid." In large part, the power of all laws comes down to whether the judicial branch of government will uphold their enforcement. So from time to time in this book, reference will be made to the problem of unenforceability of rules that are not properly promulgated. However, there may be occasions when the more general term, "valid," retains its importance. The bottom line is that any attempt by an agency to create a general standard of behavior has no legal force, unless it is through a properly created rule, or unless the agency has some exemption or exception from the rule-making process.

2. Chapter 150B, Section 18, of the North Carolina General Statutes (hereinafter G.S.).

3. These first six exemptions are full exemptions from all parts of the Administrative Procedure Act (APA) that are granted by G.S. 150B-1(c).

4. These next eight exemptions are particular exemptions from the rule-making requirements of the APA that are granted by G.S. 150B-1(d). Two additional exemptions—for the North Carolina Low-Level Radioactive Waste Management Authority in administering the provisions of G.S. 104G-10 and G.S. 104G-11 and the North Carolina Hazardous Waste Management Commission in administering the provisions of G.S. 130B-13 and G.S. 130B-14—were repealed in 2000 and 2001, respectively, as all references to those agencies and their functions were removed from the statutes.

5. The University of North Carolina is exempted from all but judicial review (Article 4 of the APA) and a particular type of contested case proceeding (construction contract claims under G.S. 143-135.3) by G.S. 150B-1(f) through December 31, 2006. After that date, the UNC system is exempted from all of the APA except judicial review.

6. Units of local government are exempted from the APA through the definition of "agency," G.S. 150B-2. However, North Carolina courts have been willing to apply the principles embodied in the APA as "highly pertinent" to review of local government actions. Coastal Ready-Mix Concrete Co. v. Board of Comm'rs of the Town of Nags Head, 299 N.C. 620, 625 (1980); Vulcan Materials Co. v. Guilford Bd. of Comm'rs., 115 N.C. App. 319 (1994). This line of decisions has been concerned only with the scope and standards of judicial review (Article 4 of the APA), not with the rule-making provisions per se. They do, however, seem to leave open arguments that principles embedded in the rule-making provisions (such as the requirements for notice through advance publication and an opportunity to comment on proposed rules) could serve as bases from which to test the legitimacy of local rule making.

7. See, e.g., G.S. 150B-1(a) ("This Chapter establishes a *uniform* system . . . ") (emphasis added).

8. See, e.g., R. BENJAMIN, ADMINISTRATIVE ADJUDICATION IN THE STATE OF NEW YORK (1942) ("much of the existing diversity [in agency procedures] exists for reasons that are not merely valid but inescapable. Thus a uniform procedure would be impossible, [even] if it were thought desirable"), quoted in A. BONFIELD, STATE ADMINISTRATIVE RULE MAKING §1.2.3, at 22–23 (Boston: Little Brown and Company, 1986) (Bonfield 1986).

9. G.S. 150B-2(8a). This definition borrows several important operative phrases from the 1961 Model State APA, but combines those phrases differently. The 1961 model language read: "'rule' means each agency statement of general applicability that implements, interprets, or prescribes law or policy, or describes the organization, or practice requirements of any agency. The term includes the amendment or repeal of a prior rule, but does not include (A) statements concerning only the internal management of an agency and not affecting private rights or procedures available to the public, or (B) declaratory rulings issued pursuant to Section 8, or (C) intra-agency memoranda." Uniform Law Commissioners' Model State Administrative Procedure Act § 1 (1961) (1961 Model State APA).

10. This tracks the 1961 Model State APA, but not the 1981 Model State APA, which adds the word "suspension" to make clear that even a temporary change of law or policy with general applicability is subject to rule making. This omission should not be given much weight in interpreting the North

Carolina statute, since the revision in the 1981 model act was intended to be merely a clarifying change. Bonfield, § 3.3.4, at 91 (1986).

11. The 1961 Model State APA contained three exclusions from the definition of "rule," including one for "statements concerning only the internal management of an agency," 1961 Model State APA §1; but in the 1981 Model State APA, these exclusions were removed from the definition of "rule" and instead were placed in Article III as special types of rules that did not have to go through the rule-making procedure. 1981 Model State APA § 3-116. North Carolina has stuck to the form of the 1961 Model Act and has continued to expand the list of exceptions to the definition of "rule" itself. The original North Carolina APA had six exclusions: the Employment Security Commission, the Industrial Commission, the Occupational Safety and Health Review Board, and the Utilities Commission for the entire APA, plus the Department of Motor Vehicles and the Department of Revenue for the rule-making and contested case provisions. G.S. 150A-1 (repealed) (1974).

12. G.S. 150B-2(8a).

13. G.S. 150B-2(8a).

14. G.S.150B-1(a).

15. The 1981 Model State APA added to the definition of "agency" a unit "created or appointed by joint or concerted action of an agency and one or more political subdivisions of the state or any of their units" in an attempt to get at this problem. 1981 MSAPA, § 1-102(1), in Bonfield, app. I at 597 (1986). North Carolina has not adopted this provision.

16. For the present rules, see 1 NCAC 38.0101 -.0603.

17. G.S. 150B-2(8a)(c).

18. The federal counterpart is at 5 U.S.C.A. § 553(b) (West 2002).

19. CHARLES E. DAYE, *North Carolina's New Administrative Procedure Act: An Interpretive Analysis*, 53 N.C. L. REV. 833, 853 (1975) (DAYE 1975).

20. DAYE 1975, citing BONFIELD, *Some Tentative Thoughts on Public Participation in the Making of Interpretive Rules and General Statements of Policy under the A.P.A.*, 23 Ad. L. Rev. 101, 108–13 (1971).

21. 1981 Model State APA § 3-109. Note that the 1981 Model State APA, unlike the North Carolina APA, does consider interpretive rules to be "rules," but it gives them a special exemption from the rule-making process.

22. *See* Chevron U.S.A. Inc., v. Natural Resources Defense Council, Inc., 467 U.S. 837, 104 S. Ct. 2778, 81 L. Ed. 2d 694 (1984); *but cf.* United States v. Mead Corp., U.S. 218, 121 S. Ct. 2164, 150 L. Ed. 2d 292 (2001).

23. *Compare* Teasley v. Beck, 155 N.C. App 282, 574 S.E.2d 137 (2002) (noting tradition of de novo review of questions of law, but citing *Chevron* and deferring to agency) *with* Jordan v. Civil Service Board, 137 N.C. App. 575 (2000), *appeal after remand*, 153 N.C. App. 691, 570 S.E.2d 912 (2002) (de novo review of questions of law requires ignoring agency interpretation). *See also* County of Durham v. North Carolina Dep't of Environment and Natural Resources, 131 N.C. App. 395, 507 S.E.2d 310 (1998) (citing *Chevron* favorably and granting deference while purportedly conducting de novo review); Thomas v. North Carolina Dep't of Human Resources, 124 N.C. App. 698, 478 S.E.2d 816 (1996) *aff'd*, 346 N.C. 268, 485 S.E.2d 295 (1997) (citing *Chevron*, but not clearly adopting its approach); Alexander v. North Carolina Dep't of Human Resources, 116 N.C. App. 15, 446 S.E.2d 847 (1994) (appearing to adopt the *Chevron* approach by giving the state

agency "great deference," albeit in interpretation of federal statute and federal regulations); Ledwell v. North Carolina Dep't of Human Resources, 114 N.C. App. 626, 442 S.E.2d 367 (1994) (citing *Chevron*, but rejecting agency interpretation at first step); Anderson v. North Carolina Dep't of Human Resources, 109 N.C. App. 680, 428 S.E.2d 267 (1993) (same); Carpenter v. North Carolina Dep't of Human Resources, 107 N.C. App. 278, 419 S.E.2d 582 (1992) (setting out but not really following *Chevron* approach). *See generally* T. Richard Kane, *Presumption of Valid Government Action— History, Scope and Impact on Burden of Proof,* A VIEW FROM THE BENCH— ADMINISTRATIVE DECISIONS (N.C. Bar Association Foundation, April 3, 2003).

24. 348 N.C. 573, 576.

25. For various judicial formulations on deference to agencies in North Carolina, see *Thorpe v. Housing Authority of City of Durham*, 89 S. Ct. 518, 393 US 268 (1969) (reversing N.C. Supreme Court decision on eviction of tenant in federally subsidized housing); *United States v. Jefferson Pilot Life Ins. Co.*, 49 F.3d 1020 (4th Cir 1995) (Court must adhere to principles of deference when reviewing agency's interpretation of its own regulation); *Clevepak Corp. v. U.S. Environmental Protection Agency*, 708 F.2d 137 (4th Cir. 1983) (deference on informal agency action, also mentioning rules obiter dictum); *Warren County v. North Carolina*, 528 F. Supp. 276 (1981); *Morrel v. Flaherty*, 338 N.C. 230, 449 S.E.2d 175 (1994) ("substantial deference"); *Winslow v. Carolina Conference Ass'n of Seventh Day Adventists*, 211 N.C. 571, 191 S.E. 403 (1937) (construction and application of rules by the Industrial Commission); *Chrysler Financial Co., LLC v. Offerman*, 138 N.C. App. 268, 531 S.E.2d 223 (2000) (due deference); *Elliot v. North Carolina Psychology Bd.*, 126 N.C. App. 453, 485 S.E.2d 882 (1997) (same), *reversed in part*, 348 N.C. 230, 498 S.E.2d 616 (1998); *Simonel v. North Caorlina School of the Arts*, 119 N.C. App. 772, 460 S.E.2d 194 (1995) (same); *Pamlico Marine Co., Inc. v. N.C. Dep't of Natural Resources and Community Development, Coastal Resources Comm'n*, 80 N.C. App. 201, 341 S.E.2d 108 (N.C. App. 1986).

26. *See, e.g.*, Food and Drug Administration v. Brown & Williamson Tobacco Corp., 529 U.S. 120, 125, 120 S. Ct. 1291, 146 L.E.2d 121 (2000).

27. *Compare* Dillingham v. North Carolina Dep't of Human Resources, 132 N.C. App. 734, 513 S.E.2d 823 (1999) (provision in agency manual requiring written evidence that a transfer of assets was made for some reason other than to establish Medicaid eligibility was a rule, creating a binding standard interpreting the eligibility requirements for Medicaid) *with* Ford v. State of North Carolina, 115 N.C. App. 556, 445 S.E.2d 425 (1994) (memorandum distributed by the Division of Alcohol Law Enforcement to its officers and the public advising of its interpretation that video poker machines violated state gambling laws did not constitute a "rule") (little discussion of administrative law provisions; note that this memorandum's ability to be accepted as a nonbinding interpretation was probably heightened by the fact that it also fit neatly under the exception for statements of audit or enforcement policy).

28. *Cf.* 56 N.C. Atty. Gen. Op. 25, 28 (1986) ("any procedures, whether formal or informal, that directly or substantially affect the rights or procedures of non-agency persons must be adopted as rules.")

29. *See* 26 NCAC 02C.0205.

30. G.S. 150B-21.19(1) (authority); 26 NCAC 02C .0406 (history note).

31. G.S. 150B-21.21. The codifier has issued rules for numbering and arranging rules in the North Carolina Administrative Code (NCAC); these are set out at 26 NCAC 2C.0201 to 2C.0207. To illustrate the above answer on the scope of a "rule," there are seven separate rules within this codification section of the NCAC: Rules .0201, .0202, .0203, .0204, .0205, .0206, and .0207.

32. *Compare* G.S. 150A-10 and 150A-11 (repealed) *with* G.S. 150A-58 (repealed). *See also* GREGORY WALLACE, THE ATTORNEY GENERAL'S MANUAL ON RULE MAKING AND FILING AT 1 (Raleigh: N.C. Dep't of Justice, 1980).

33. Rules not only have the force of law, *see, e.g., Westmoreland v. Laird*, 364 F. Supp. 948, *aff'd* 485 F.2d 1237 (1973), they also may alter the common law. *In re* Declaratory Ruling by North Carolina Comm'r of Insurance Regarding 11 NCAC 12.0319, 134 N.C. App. 22 (1999).

34. *See* G.S. 150B-1(a) ("This Chapter establishes a uniform system of administrative rule making and adjudicatory procedures for agencies. The procedures ensure that the functions of rule making, investigation, advocacy, and adjudication are not all performed by the same person in the administrative process").

35. For a good summary of the differences, see BONFIELD 1986, at §2.1.2–2.1.3, 30–39.

36. G.S. 150B-2(1a).

37. BONFIELD 1986, §2.2.1 at 42–43 1986.

38. *See supra* note 15 (hybrid form covered by 1981 MSAPA).

39. G.S. 150-19 (formerly G.S. 150B-9). *See* General Motors Corp. v. Kinlaw, 78 N.C. App. 521, 338 S.E.2d 114 (1985).

40. 328 N.C. 456, 464 (1991). Professor Bonfield would allow a claim to direct constitutional authority: "agencies may only exercise those powers expressly or impliedly delegated to them by the legislature, or in rare cases, by the state constitution." [citing 1 AM. JUR. 2d *Administrative Law* sec. 70 (1962)] BONFIELD 1986, § 5.2.1 at 144.

41. General Motors Corp. v. Kinlaw, 78 N.C. App 521, 530 (1985).

42. G.S. 150B-19(2).

43. G.S. 150B-19(3).

44. G.S. 150B-19(4).

45. G.S. 150B-19(5).

46. G.S. 150B-19(6).

47. *Cf.* James v. Sutton, 229 N.C. 515 (1948) (the statutory zoning power of governing body of municipality cannot be delegated to board of adjustment and board cannot permit a type of business or building prohibited by a zoning ordinance, for to do so would be an amendment of the law and not a variance of board's regulations).

48. 293 U.S. 388 (1935).

49. 295 U.S. 495 (1935).

50. Even some early cases, both federal and in North Carolina, conceded the importance of giving broad delegated power to agencies: "The Constitution does not deny to Congress necessary resources of flexibility and practicality which will enable it to perform its function in laying down policies and establishing standards while leaving to selected instrumentalities the making of subordinate rules within prescribed limits and determination of facts to which

policy as declared by Legislature is to apply." Currin v. Wallace, 306 U.S. 1 (1939). *See also* Motsinger v. Perryman, 218 N.C. 15 (1940) (the authority to make rules and regulations to carry out an express legislative purpose or to effect the operation and enforcement of a law is not an exclusively "legislative power" but is "administrative" in its nature and may be delegated by the legislature).

51. Whitman v. American Trucking Associations, 531 U.S. 457, 121 S. Ct. 903, 149 L. Ed. 2d 1, (2001).

52. KENNETH C. DAVIS, TREATISE at 3.14 (1978). Professor Davis traces this evolution further in the federal courts: Beginning in 1980, with *Industrial Union Department, AFL-CIO v. American Petroleum Institute*, 448 U.S. 607 (1980), and *American Textile Manufacturers Institute, Inc. v. Donovan*, 452 U.S. 490 (1981) (cotton dust case), the U.S. Supreme Court has been willing to uphold rules even when it believes Congress has not determined the ultimate policy. *See* DAVIS, SUPPLEMENT TO ADMINISTRATIVE LAW TREATISE sec. 3:1 at 54–58 (1989). On this theory, the chief executive may provide the needed guidance for exercise of major policymaking power. North Carolina has not yet gone this far.

53. *See* Spruce Pine v. Avery County, 346 N.C. 787, 488 S.E.2d 144 (1997); Adams v. N.C. Department of Natural and Economic Resources, 295 N.C. 683, 249 S.E.2d 402 (1978).

54. *See also In Re* Community Association, 300 N.C. 267, 273 (1980) (denial of dredge and fill permit not a violation of nondelegation doctrine based on legislative standard of "significant adverse effect on the value and enjoyment of the property of any riparian owners").

55. *Compare* G.S. 146-1(a) ("rules and regulations adopted by the Governor") *with* G.S. 146-2 ("The Department of Administration shall . . . subject to the approval of the Governor and Council of State . . . adopt such rules and regulations as it may deem necessary"). Slight conflicts such as this make no real difference where the reporting relationship is clear: the secretary of administration reports to and serves at the pleasure of the governor, so whether the primary rule-making responsibility is in the governor's office or the secretary's office does not matter much. This type of ambiguity is much more problematic if the authority is arguably vested in two different places with two different reporting and oversight lines.

56. *See* Randolph v. United States, 274 F. Supp. 200 (M.D.N.C. 1967), *aff'd*, 389 U.S. 570, 88 S. Ct 695, 19 L. Ed. 2d 785 (1968) (refusing to invalidate a Social Security Administration regulation relating to maximum attorney fees for prosecution of claims before administration due to delegation by Secretary of Health, Education, and Welfare); State *ex rel.* Comm'r of Ins. v. North Carolina Rate Bureau, 300 N.C. 381, 269 S.E.2d 547 (1980). *But see* Matter of Broad and Gales Creek Community Ass'n, 300 N.C. 267, 266 S.E.2d 645 (1980) (need to delegate legislative powers to use administrative expertise must be reconciled with constitutional mandate that legislature retain in its own hands the supreme legislative power; the supreme court must insure that decision making by an administrative agency is not arbitrary and unreasoned and that the agency is not asked to make important policy choices that might just as easily be made by the legislature, noting the separation of powers clause of the North Carolina Constitution. The seminal *Adams* case

recognizes that a modern legislature must be able to delegate problems with complex conditions and numerous details. Adams v. North Carolina Dep't of Natural and Economic Resources, 295 N.C. 683 (1978).

57. President John F. Kennedy, 107 Cong. Rec. 5847, 5849 (1961). Davis notes that the following decades saw a sharp drop in successful challenges to agency action on the grounds of improper subdelegation.

58. But see *Shook v. District of Columbia Financial Responsibility and Management Assistance Authority*, 132 F.3d 775 (D.C. Dir. 1998), and Halverson v. Slater, 129 F.3d 180 (D.C. Cir. 1997), suggesting a new, more skeptical approach to subdelegation at the federal level.

59. *Cf.* Perot v. FEC, 97 F.3d 553 (D.C. Cir. 1996) (rejecting argument that the Federal Election Commission had delegated authority to the Commission on Presidential Debates).

60. G.S. 143B-9.

61. G.S. 143B-10(a).

62. 26 NCAC 02C.0403(b).

63. N.C. Const. art. III, § 10. *But see* G.S. 143A-8 (noting the governor's power to reorganize "except as otherwise expressly provided by statute").

64. Comm'r of Insurance v. Rate Bureau, 300 N.C. 381 (1980).

65. G.S. 150B-2(1c).

66. G.S. 150B-21.18.

67. G.S. 150B-21.22.

68. G.S. 150B-21.17.

69. G.S. 150B-21.17(a).

70. *See* G.S. 150B-21.17(b). These requirements are set out in more detail in the section of this book on the form of proposed rules, pages 36 to 38.

71. *See* Southern Railway v. O'Boyle Tank Lines, 70 N.C. App. 1 (1984).

72. *See* G.S. 150B-21.21.

73. G.S. 150B-21.21(a), (b).

74. G.S. 150B-21.21(b).

Chapter 2

How does the rule-making process work?

If any one thing is clear about the rule-making process for state agencies in North Carolina, it is that the process is in constant flux. With luck, changes in the process will not dramatically affect a particular rule. Legislative proposals for change in the Administrative Procedure Act (APA) were introduced in nearly every session since the major revisions of 1995. Yet another major revision passed in 2003. Such major reforms have been made every decade in the 1970s, 1980s, 1990s, and 2000s. Thus readers who want to ensure the current validity of the process outlined below need to consult legislative summaries for any sessions since the publication of this book.[1]

As noted at the outset of this book, a rule of an agency covered by the APA rule-making provisions is not valid or enforceable unless it is adopted in substantial compliance with the APA rule-making process. Rules have been struck down by the courts for not going through this process.[2] Note that some agencies have administrative law–like procedures (such as requirements for notice and comment on agency actions) built into their organic statutes. These are normally best understood as complements to, rather than substitutes for, the APA provisions. An agency must fulfill its statutory obligations under both sets of procedural requirements; conversely, exemption from one set of requirements does not in and of itself imply exemption from the other set.[3]

Emergency rules

The process for making emergency rules is completely different from the process for temporary and permanent rules. The process for emergency rules is simple and quick; the process for temporary and permanent rules is comparatively complex and long. The concept of "emergency rules" was reintroduced by the 2003 changes to the APA. The term "emergency rule" has actually been around state administrative rule making since the 1961 Model Rules. Prior to 2003 in North Carolina, however, the process now used for "emergency" rules was applied to "temporary" rules. In other words, between the 1980s and the changes in 2003, when the legislature revived the concept of "emergency rules," a "temporary" rule had the advantage of essentially the same simple promulgation process that "emergency" rules now have. Accordingly, agencies (and the legislature, for rules it favored) were always looking for ways to adopt rules as temporary rules, if at all possible. The 2003 changes were motivated, in large part, by the legislature's desire to cut down on the number of rules going into effect with the minimal process now required for "emergency" rules. Early indications are that this policy change has accomplished its goal.[4]

What qualifies for emergency rule making? In addition to the basic rule-making authority required for any rule, an agency wishing to adopt an emergency rule must show that following the normal, permanent rule-making process would be "contrary to the public interest" and that "the immediate adoption of the rule is required by "a serious and unforeseen threat to the public health or safety."[5] Note the absence of a "threat to public welfare" criterion for emergency rules, in contrast to temporary rules. Note also that the Department of Health and Human Services, or its appropriate subagency, can adopt emergency rules to provide increased services or benefits when a recent legislative change has allowed such an increase.[6]

This showing is made to the codifier of rules in the form of a "statement of need." The codifier reviews the required "written statement of its findings by the head of the agency adopting the [emergency] rule."[7] The codifier of rules has two business days from receipt of the proposed emergency rule to determine whether it meets the "serious and unforeseen threat to public health" criterion.[8] The codifier is also directed to publish the proposed emergency rule on the Internet within five business days.[9]

The process for emergency rules When the codifier of rules decides that a statement of need for an emergency rule is adequate, judged against the standards set out above, the rule must be entered in the North Carolina Administrative Code

(NCAC) on the sixth business day following approval.[10] It is effective as soon as it is entered into the NCAC.[11] Thus the emergency rule-making process can be very simple. When an emergency rule is entered into the NCAC, it must also be published in the *North Carolina Register*.[12]

Although the codifier of rules is given the power to review proposed emergency rules and to ask for more information bolstering the "statement of need," if the agency refuses to supply that information, the emergency rule will go into effect anyway. It simply is delayed until the sixth business day after the codifier receives notice that the agency refuses to give new or additional information.[13]

Emergency rules have a very limited life, which is (at most) sixty days from the date of publication in the *North Carolina Register*.[14] However, if the agency has submitted a temporary rule to replace the emergency rule to the Rules Review Commission, this sixty-day period is tolled and the emergency rule will stay in place pending action on the temporary rule.[15] The provisions for limited life of emergency and temporary rules are designed to force an agency into beginning and carrying out the permanent rule-making process in reasonably expeditious fashion. Some agencies have attempted to extend the lives of temporary rules indefinitely by replacing them with new temporary rules. This clearly violates the letter and spirit of the expiration provisions for emergency rules.[16] An emergency rule will end earlier than sixty days if it so provides in the rule, or if either a temporary rule is adopted to replace it or a proposed temporary rule intended to replace it is disapproved by the Rules Review Commission.[17] It will end later than sixty days only if the replacement permanent rule has been submitted to the Rules Review Commission but not yet been acted on, or if legislative authority has been given outside the APA (such as in an organic statute) for a longer emergency rule duration.

Duration of emergency rules

Figure 2-1 is a flow chart of the emergency rule-making process prepared by the Office of Administrative Hearings shortly after passage of the 2003 APA reforms.

Temporary rules

The process for making temporary rules is, after the 2003 changes, not dramatically different from the process for permanent rules. The main process differences are shorter time periods for notice, comment, and review and less required pre-rule consultation and analysis.

Figure 2-1.
Emergency Rule Making
(G.S. 150B - 21.1A)

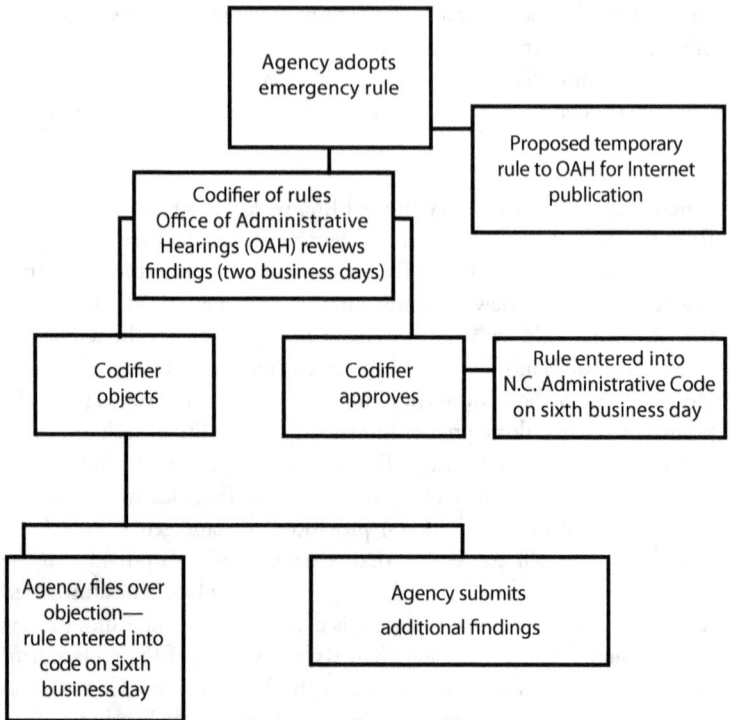

```
                    ┌─────────────────────┐
                    │   Agency adopts      │
                    │   emergency rule     ├──────┐
                    └──────────┬───────────┘      │
                               │         ┌─────────────────────────┐
                               │         │   Proposed temporary     │
                               │         │   rule to OAH for Internet│
                               │         │   publication            │
                               │         └─────────────────────────┘
              ┌────────────────┴──────────────┐
              │   Codifier of rules           │
              │   Office of Administrative     │
              │   Hearings (OAH) reviews       │
              │   findings (two business days) │
              └───────┬───────────────┬───────┘
                      │               │
         ┌────────────┴───┐   ┌───────┴──────┐   ┌─────────────────────────┐
         │   Codifier     │   │   Codifier    │   │   Rule entered into      │
         │   objects      │   │   approves    │   │   N.C. Administrative Code│
         └───────┬────────┘   └──────────────┘   │   on sixth business day  │
                 │                                 └─────────────────────────┘
      ┌──────────┴──────────────────────────────┐
      │                                          │
┌─────┴────────────┐              ┌──────────────┴──────────┐
│ Agency files over │              │   Agency submits         │
│ objection—        │              │   additional findings    │
│ rule entered into │              │                          │
│ code on sixth     │              └──────────────────────────┘
│ business day      │
└───────────────────┘
```

Emergency rule expires on the earliest of the following dates:

1. The date specified in the rule.
2. The effective date of the temporary rule adopted to replace the emergency rule, if the Rules Review Commission approves the temporary rule.
3. The date the Commission returns to an agency a temporary rule the agency adopted to replace the emergency rule.
4. Sixty days from the date the emergency rule was published in the *North Carolina Register*, unless the temporary rule adopted to replace the emergency rule has been submitted to the Commission.

Note: This document is based on one prepared by the Office of Administrative Hearings as a public service and is not to be deemed binding or controlling. (09/02/03)

In addition to the basic rule-making authority required for any rule, an agency wishing to adopt a temporary rule must show that following the normal, permanent rule-making process would be

What qualifies for temporary rule making?

> contrary to the public interest and that the immediate adoption of the rule is required by one or more of the following:
>
> (1) A serious and unforeseen threat to the public health, safety or welfare.
> (2) The effective date of a recent act of the General Assembly or the United States Congress.
> (3) A recent change in federal or State budgetary policy.
> (4) A federal regulation.
> (5) A court order.[18]

This showing is made in the form of a "statement of need" signed by the agency head and eventually reviewed by the Rules Review Commission. At least thirty days prior to adoption of the temporary rule, the agency must submit the text of the proposed rule and a notice of public hearing to the codifier of rules. The codifier publishes the proposed temporary rule and the notice of public hearing on the Internet[19] within five business days. The agency is simultaneously required to notify persons on its mailing list "and any other interested parties" of its intent to adopt temporary rules and of its public hearing.[20] The agency is required to accept written comments on the proposed temporary rule for at least fifteen business days prior to adoption and to hold at least one public hearing no less than five business days after the rule and notice have been published.[21]

When the agency adopts the temporary rule, it submits it and the written statement of need, signed by the head of the agency, to the Rules Review Commission.[22] The Rules Review Commission must review the statement of need and the rule within fifteen business days and either approve it and deliver it to the codifier, or else return it to the agency as "not approved."[23] In order to provide this expedited review, the statute directs the Rules Review Commission to have a staff attorney review the rule and make a recommendation either to the full commission or to a panel of at least three members of the commission, which panel is authorized to act for the commission on proposed temporary rules.[24]

The Rules Review Commission, or its designee, reviews a temporary rule not only for whether it makes the required showing of need for a rule, but also for all the standards required of permanent rules: authority, clarity, necessity, and procedure.[25] These review standards for temporary rules were another new feature of the rule-making process introduced by the 2003 reforms; prior to those changes, there was no review outside of the agency of the content or authority for a temporary rule.

One of the statutory bases of need for temporary rules, the "recent act" provision, was defined by the legislature in the 2003 APA changes to mean an effective date no more than 210 days prior to submission of a temporary rule to the Rules Review Commission.[26] Thus an agency wishing to make a temporary rule change in response to a change in a statute has a fairly narrow window of time (seven months) to draft and submit the language, absent one of the special legislative provisions circumventing this deadline.[27]

The process for temporary rules

When the Rules Review Commission, or its designated panel, decides that a statement of need for a temporary rule is adequate and the rule itself meets the standards of G.S. 150B-21.9, the rule must be delivered to the codifier of rules within two business days of approval.[28] The codifier of rules must enter it into the NCAC on the sixth business day following receipt from the commission.[29] It is effective as soon as it is entered into the code.[30] When a temporary rule is entered into the code, it must also be published in the *North Carolina Register.*[31]

If the Rules Review Commission or its designee finds the statement of need or the rule itself defective, it must return the rule to the agency, which then may provide additional information. This back and forth can go on until the agency gives up attempting to satisfy the objections of the Rules Review Commission, at which point the temporary rule is dead. The agency's recourse is to file an action for declaratory judgment in Wake County Superior Court, if it believes the Rules Review Commission has erred in its judgment on the proposed rule.[32]

Duration of temporary rules

Temporary rules have a limited life, which is (at the most) 270 days from the date of publication in the *North Carolina Register.*[33] However, if the agency has submitted a permanent rule to replace the temporary rule to the Rules Review Commission, this 270-day period is tolled and the temporary rule will stay in place pending action on the permanent rule.[34] The provisions for limited life of a temporary rule are designed to force an agency into beginning and carrying out the permanent rule-making process in reasonably expeditious fashion. Some agencies have attempted to extend the lives of temporary rules indefinitely by replacing them with new temporary rules. This clearly violates the letter and spirit of the expiration provisions for temporary rules.[35] A temporary rule will end earlier than 270 days if it so provides in the rule, or if either a permanent rule is adopted to replace it or a proposed permanent rule intended to replace it is disapproved by the Rules Review Commission or the legislature.[36] It will end later than 270 days only if the replacement permanent rule has been submitted to the Rules Review Commission, but not yet been acted on, or if legislative authority has been given outside the APA (such as in an organic statute) for a longer temporary rule duration.

As noted above, with the great rise in complexity and delay of permanent rule making caused by the 1995 amendments to the APA, there has been a correspondingly great push to special provisions for temporary rule making. In addition, at least two agencies, the Wildlife Resources Commission and the Marine Fisheries Commission, already had some special form of rule making–like power that allowed quick changes in their laws. These special provisions and special forms are noted below.

The Wildlife Resources Commission is authorized in the APA to adopt a temporary rule to establish no-wake zones, hunting or fishing seasons, hunting or fishing bag limits, or management rules for public game lands.[37] The Wildlife Resources Commission is also permitted to issue "proclamations" concerning many matters within its jurisdiction and to delegate this authority to its executive director. This proclamation authority operates with minimal process and outside the APA.[38] The Marine Fisheries Commission, and by delegation the Fisheries director, has functionally similar authority to make "proclamations" regarding marine fisheries limits and the opening and closing of seasons.[39]

Other offices that have received special exceptions to the normal process for temporary rules include

- The secretary of state, to implement a technology certification process[40]
- The commissioner of insurance, to implement the provisions of Chapter 58, Section 2-205 of the North Carolina General Statutes (hereinafter G.S.)[41]
- The secretary of commerce, to implement information technology procurement provisions[42]
- The State Board of Elections, for almost anything it regulates[43]

Many other agencies have received special dispensation, since 1995, for temporary rule making. This area of the APA best illustrates the fraying of uniformity in the administrative rule-making process in the late 1990s.

The 2003 changes to the temporary and permanent rule-making process were designed to increase the difficulty of creating temporary rules, and to decrease the agencies' perceived need for them, by streamlining the permanent rule-making process for "noncontroversial" rules. Whether these changes will also stem the tide of special exceptions to the normal APA process is as yet unclear.

Figure 2-2 is a flow chart of the temporary rule-making process prepared by the Office of Administrative Hearings shortly after passage of the 2003 APA reforms.

Figure 2-2.
Temporary Rule Making
(G.S. 150B - 21.1)

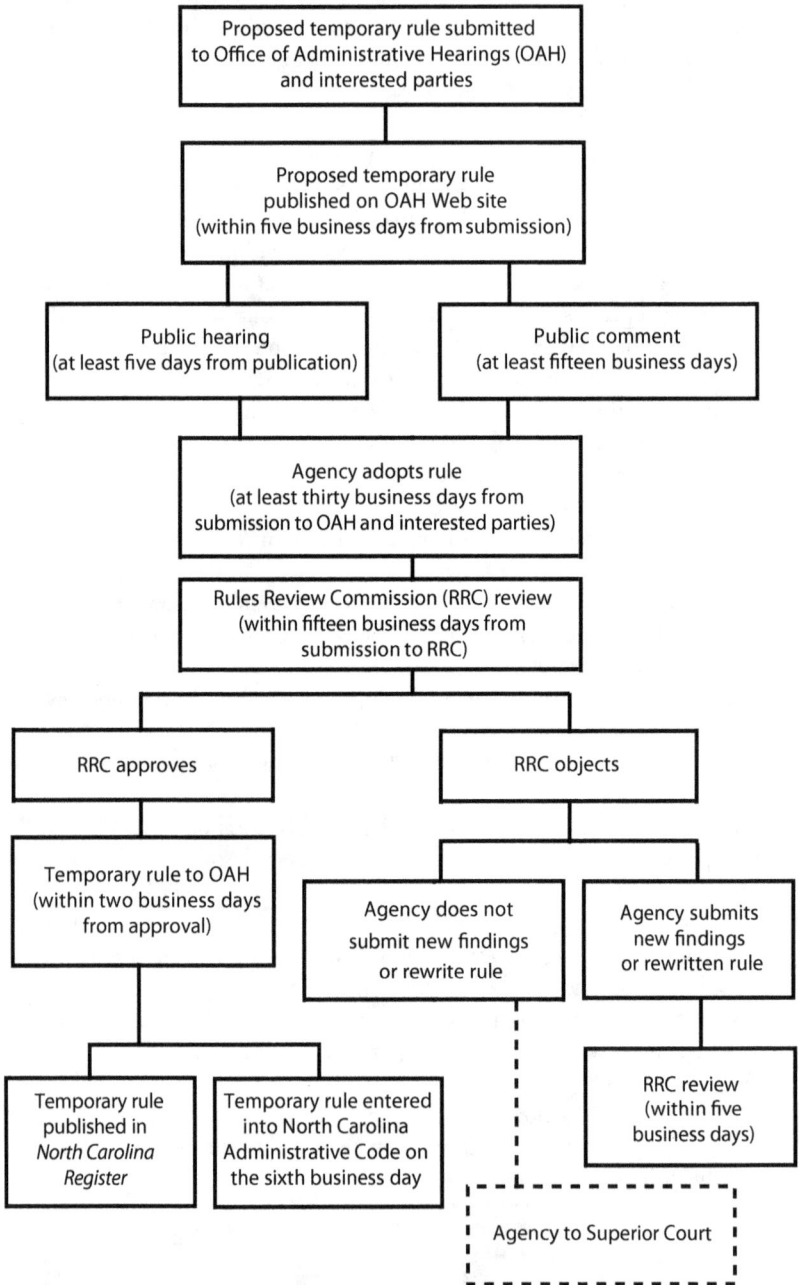

Proposed temporary rule submitted
to Office of Administrative Hearings (OAH)
and interested parties

Proposed temporary rule
published on OAH Web site
(within five business days from submission)

Public hearing
(at least five days from publication)

Public comment
(at least fifteen business days)

Agency adopts rule
(at least thirty business days from
submission to OAH and interested parties)

Rules Review Commission (RRC) review
(within fifteen business days from
submission to RRC)

RRC approves

RRC objects

Temporary rule to OAH
(within two business days
from approval)

Agency does not
submit new findings
or rewrite rule

Agency submits
new findings
or rewritten rule

Temporary rule
published in
*North Carolina
Register*

Temporary rule entered
into North Carolina
Administrative Code on
the sixth business day

RRC review
(within five
business days)

Agency to Superior Court

Note: This document is based on a document prepared by the Office of Administrative
Hearings as a public service and is not to be deemed binding or controlling. (10/07/03)

Permanent rules: Internal agency drafting and analysis steps

Rules that do not qualify as emergency or temporary rules are called "permanent rules." They are subject to the full rule-making process, which is described in the General Statutes in G.S. 150B-21.2 through 150B-21.16, unless they fall into one of several narrow categories that do not require notice and comment. These exceptions are discussed below. The steps in the process can usefully be grouped into three stages:

1. the internal agency (particularly agency staff) steps taken in drafting and analyzing a rule before it is given public notice and sent out for formal comment;
2. the formal notice, comment, and deliberation steps taken by agencies (particularly agency heads and commissions) in deciding whether and in what form to propose a final rule; and
3. the executive branch, rules review, and legislative oversight steps necessary before a proposed rule becomes the law.

Each of these stages is discussed separately below, starting with the internal agency steps taken in drafting and analyzing a rule. The permanent rule-making process as presently constituted is a long one, although reforms made in 2003 were intended to speed up the process for most rules. It can take as long as eighteen months for a rule objected to by someone to be created or changed in North Carolina.[44]

There are nine types of rule changes an agency can make without being required to publish notices and hold hearings or otherwise accept comment. The agency can change its rules without notice or comment to

Rule changes that do not require notice and comment

(1) Reletter or renumber a rule or its subparts.
(2) Substitute one name for another when an organization or position is renamed.
(3) Correct a citation in the rule to another rule or law when the citation changes due to repeal or renumbering.
(4) Change information that is readily available to the public, such as an address or a telephone number.
(5) Correct a typographical error in the NCAC.
(6) Change a rule in response to a request or an objection by the commission, unless the commission determines that the change is substantial.[45]

This last item is discussed further in the section on Rules Review Commission review, below.

In the following circumstances, an agency can repeal a rule without going through the notice and comment process

(7) The law under which the rule was adopted is repealed.

(8) The law under which the rule was adopted or the rule itself is declared unconstitutional.

(9) The rule is declared to be in excess of the agency's statutory authority.[46]

The Occupational Safety and Health Division of the Department of Labor also has a special exception allowing it to adopt an occupational safety and health standard that is identical to a federal regulation of the Department of Labor without notice, comment, or submission to the Rules Review Commission.[47]

Rules can be reordered or otherwise revised as to form by the codifier of rules within ten business days of their submission for codification without going through the whole process for rule changes.[48] But when an agency has a need to recodify or otherwise reorganize large portions of rules—for example, when there is a major restructuring of executive branch departments—there must be express authority from the legislature to allow the reorganization of rules without going through the entire APA process.[49]

Pre-draft consultation with interested parties

The clear trend in rule making over the period from the 1980s to the present, at least in areas where rules have significant economic consequences, is for agencies to view the APA notice and comment requirements as the minimum required and to seek further and less formal means of consultation with interested parties before the text of proposed rules is published. As at the federal level, many forms and variations of this pre-draft consultation have been tried, from formal regulatory negotiations to phone calls by agency staff to persons known to be interested in the rules. The APA itself does not require broadly representative pre-draft consultation, but this type of effort is generally good practice for rules that have significant consequences.

The APA does require pre-draft consultation with representatives of local government—the North Carolina Association of County Commissioners, the North Carolina League of Municipalities, and samples of county managers or city managers as appropriate, when rule making might

1. Require any unit of local government, including entities funded by or through local government, to carry out additional or modified responsibilities;

2. Increase the costs of public services funded in whole or part by any unit of local government; or

3. Otherwise affect the expenditures or revenues of a unit of local government.

These consultation efforts are supposed to be led by the agency's rule-making coordinator, who is supposed to report directly to the agency head.[50] To mitigate the intrusiveness of this requirement in an agency that wishes to deploy its rule-making and negotiations expertise differently, it is possible to appoint more than one "rule-making coordinator" in an agency.[51]

The Governor's Office has, from time to time, issued executive orders or taken less formal means to require cabinet agencies to consult with interested parties in advance of rule making. One effect of the analytical requirements imposed on rule making agencies by the 1995 APA amendments is that it will often be necessary to consult with interested parties to gather the data necessary to prepare fiscal notes.

Drafting rules

It takes great skill and ability to draft good rules. A rule is a bit of law, and laws have real consequences, such as the loss of a person's property or liberty. The language embodying the law is likely to be tested, perhaps in a lawsuit which itself will have significant outcomes. Just as with legislative drafting, entire programs can be made or lost and good intentions can be implemented or ignored as a result of choices made in drafting. These significant consequences argue for precision in rule language. However, the desire for precision often rubs against the equally important need for clarity. To be complied with, a rule must be understood. In many cases, state administrative rules will be drafted by persons with little or no prior training or experience in legal drafting, and they will be interpreted and responded to by persons with little or no training in legal interpretation. The art of rule drafting is the art of attaining clear precision: maximum enforceability as well as maximum understandability. As an art, rule drafting is beyond the scope of this book. However, a few style issues and many formatting requirements are discussed below.

One common and egregious error in rule drafting is assuming that the legal power of a rule is somehow related to the use of "legalese." In other words, the drafter writes as if the way the words sound is more important than what they mean. In fact, just the opposite is true. The more legalistic filler words, extra syllables, passive voice, antique phrases, and arcane constructions in a rule, the less likely it is that the real intent of the language will be understood and acted on by persons affected by the rule. Avoid legalese. Strive for plain English. Avoid passive voice. Use active sentences.

Incorporation by reference

The APA specifically allows the incorporation of certain material in a rule by reference:

(1) Another rule or part of a rule adopted by the agency.

(2) All or part of a code, standard, or regulation adopted by another agency, the federal government, or a generally recognized organization or association.[52]

However, the incorporation by reference must state whether it incorporates subsequent amendments and editions of the referenced material. The agency must also keep copies of the incorporated material available for inspection and must state in the rule where those copies can be obtained and the cost (on the date the rule is adopted) of a copy of the material.[53]

Older rules that incorporated material by reference sometimes used a citation to former sections of the APA, now repealed. Material incorporated under former G.S. 150B-14(b) does not include subsequent amendments and editions; material incorporated under former G.S. 150B-14(c) does include subsequent amendments and editions.[54]

Format issues

The Office of Administrative Hearings maintains a handout and materials on its Web site, www.oah.state.nc.us, with current guidelines on formatting rules. Since the Office of Administrative Hearings can refuse to publish and codify rules that do not meet its requirements,[55] it is worth paying attention to the current guidelines. There are also rules for formatting rules at 26 NCAC 02C.0100 *et seq.* and other formatting matters are addressed elsewhere in subchapter 2C of the North Carolina Administrative Code.

These rules and guidelines may seem like impediments to efficient rule making to rule drafters in a given agency; but to everyone other than the drafters (who have in their mind what the rule language is supposed to mean and accomplish), the formatting guidelines greatly simplify the problem of reading a proposed rule and understanding what is new and different about it, what is legally important, and what the rule's history and authority are. By following the "Rule Format Checklist," an agency can be reasonably assured that it is also meeting the requirements of subchapter 2C, as regards rule format.

Exhibit 2-1 is an example of an actual rule with a subchapter heading preceding it.

Exhibit 2-1.
Example of Rule with Subchapter Heading Preceding It

NORTH CAROLINA ADMINISTRATIVE CODE
TITLE 26. OFFICE OF ADMINISTRATIVE HEARINGS
CHAPTER 02. RULES DIVISION
SUBCHAPTER 2C—SUBMISSION PROCEDURES FOR RULES AND OTHER DOCUMENTS TO BE PUBLISHED IN THE NORTH CAROLINA REGISTER AND THE NORTH CAROLINA ADMINISTRATIVE CODE

SECTION .0100 - GENERAL
Current with rules received through October 29, 2004

26 NCAC 02C .0101   SCOPE

(a) The rules in this Section set forth the general requirements for an agency to submit rules and documents for publication.

(b) For notices and rules submitted for publication in the Register, the agency shall also comply with the requirements set out in Sections .0200 and .0300 of this Subchapter.

(c) For a rule submitted for inclusion in the Code that was noticed in the Register, an agency shall also comply with the requirements set out in Section .0400 of this Subchapter.

(d) For a rule submitted for inclusion in the Code and the rule was not noticed in the Register, an agency shall also comply with the requirements set out in Sections .0200 and .0400 of this Subchapter.

(e) For a temporary rule submitted for publication in the Register and the Code, an agency shall also comply with the requirements set out in Sections .0200 through .0500 of this Subchapter.

(f) For a rule submitted for publication on the OAH website, an agency shall also comply with the requirements set out in Sections .0200 and .0700 of this Subchapter.

(g) For an emergency rule submitted for review and publication in the Register and Code, an agency shall also comply with the requirements set out in Sections .0200 and .0600 of this Subchapter.

History Note: Authority G.S. 150B-21.17; 150B-21.18; 150B-21.19;
*   Temporary Amendment Eff. July 1, 2003;*
*   Amended Eff. April 1, 2004.*

The subchapter and section headings are for convenience of searching only and should not be written as if they have legal significance. The same is true of the catch line for the rule, the rule number, and the citation.[56]

The line spacing and indentation shown above are required to be followed in rules.[57] The history note should be formatted exactly as shown, in italics, with a recitation of authority and an effective date. For help in constructing a rule's history, or help with any formatting issues in the drafting stage, call an agency's rule coordinator or the Rules Division of the Office of Administrative Hearings.[58]

The 1995 analytical requirements: Fiscal notes, federal mandates, and local impacts

A major revision of the APA rule-making requirements in 1995 introduced a "veto" over rules by the Rules Review Commission and increased requirements to analyze and minimize the impact of proposed rules. These analytical requirements reflected the trend at the time to "regulatory reform" in the manner of cost-benefit analysis and other attempts to require consideration of the costs of rules, as well as their benefits.[59] Critics charged that these requirements were really about "paralysis by analysis," that is, slowing down or stopping the rule-making process rather than a genuine interest in assessing the costs and benefits of rules. The compromise that emerged in North Carolina in 1995 required creation of a "fiscal note" for certain rules as well as heightened attention to the impacts of rules on local government.

Prior to 1995, the APA already contained a requirement for preparation of a fiscal note when a proposed rule involved the spending or distribution of state funds. This type of fiscal note, which is still required, is aimed at projecting the amount of state funds required by a rule and involves a certification by the Office of State Budget and Management that adequate funds are available.[60]

The APA now also requires that an agency consider whether a proposed rule would affect the expenditures or revenues of a unit of local government. If so, a fiscal note must be prepared, showing the amount of impact on local revenues and expenditures, and must be submitted with the text of the proposed rule to the Governor's Office for a minimum thirty-day review.[61] The fiscal note and text also must go to the Fiscal Research Division of the General Assembly, the Office of State Budget and Management, the North Carolina Association of County Commissioners, and the North Carolina League of Municipalities.[62] Furthermore, the APA now requires that agencies proposing rules that would increase or decrease the expenditures or revenues of a unit of local government must consider the timing of the effective date of those rules; and if the rule would "disrupt the budget process," the agency is directed to set the effective date as July 1 following the date the rule would otherwise become effective.[63] This is intended to allow changes to be factored into local government budgeting, with fiscal years beginning on July 1.

Another trigger that requires preparation of a fiscal note is a proposed rule that is expected to have an aggregate financial impact on all persons affected of at least $3 million in a year.[64] A rule with this degree of "substantial economic impact" and that is not identical to a federal regulation the agency is required to adopt must be analyzed, either by the agency, with approval from the Office of State Budget and Management, or by the Office of State Budget and Management itself. The Office of State Budget and Management has ninety days from receipt of a written request to prepare the fiscal note; if it misses that deadline, an agency can prepare the note itself and is not required to get approval for it from the Office of State Budget and Management. Otherwise an agency that prepares its own "substantial economic impact" fiscal note must submit it to the Office of State Budget and Management, which is supposed to review the note within fourteen days.[65]

The APA spells out the content requirements for a "substantial economic impact" fiscal note:

(1) A description of the persons who would be affected by the proposed rule change;
(2) A description of the types of expenditures that persons affected by the proposed rule change would have to make to comply with the rule, along with an estimate of those expenditures;
(3) A description of the purpose and benefits of the proposed rule change; and
(4) An explanation of how the expenditure estimate was calculated.[66]

The statute expressly provides that errors in fiscal notes prepared in good faith do not affect the validity of a rule.[67]

For rules that are purportedly required to be adopted to implement a federal law, or to maintain compliance with federal law, or to receive federal funds, the rule-making coordinator is required to prepare a certificate identifying the relevant federal law and explaining why the state rule is required and whether it exceeds the requirements of federal law. The federal compliance certificate should not include comments on the merits of the proposed rule.[68]

Permanent rules: Formal notice, comment, deliberation, and adoption of rules

Agency deliberation steps

Agencies differ greatly in the steps they take to get approval of proposed rules internally, before sending out the proposed text for formal notice and comment. Some agency heads or commission members may be involved closely in the early discussion and drafting stages and in informal comments and negotiations with stakeholders. Other agency heads and commission members may have little idea what a rule is about or why it is being considered until the agency staff members have already produced a draft text and done any required analysis. This is just the nature of rule making and of agencies: they both vary widely in size, complexity, and need for early senior management involvement. As noted above, the agency with authority to issue the rule could be a department, within or outside the governor's cabinet, or it could be an appointed commission made up of part-time volunteers. The actual person or persons responsible for giving the final authorization to proceed could be a secretary of a department, someone with a delegation from a secretary of a department,[69] or a group of commission members. Whatever the steps involved, there comes a time when the proper person must authorize the publication of a proposed rule's text and any accompanying fiscal note.

Notice of text

Once an agency decides it wants to create or change a rule, other than making one of the nine narrow changes noted above, and determines that it has authority to do so, its first formal step on the path is publication of a "notice of text."[70] Publication is made in the *North Carolina Register* and by mailing the notice to everyone on the mailing list required to be kept by statute.[71] Publishing this notice requires an agency to begin to accept written and oral comments on the proposed rule making.

The text of the proposed rule must first be published in the *North Carolina Register* (with a copy sent to persons on the rule-making mailing list), following the format guidelines referenced above. Several statutory requirements apply to this publication; it must include all of the following:

(1) The text of the proposed rule.
(2) A short explanation of the reason for the proposed rule.
(3) A citation to the authority for the rule (in the history section).
(4) The proposed effective date of the rule.
(5) The date, time and place of any public hearings scheduled on the rule.

(6) Instructions on how a person can demand a public hearing, if one is not already scheduled and the rule is subject to a public hearing demand.

(7) The time period and person to receive written comments.

(8) If there is a fiscal note, a statement noting that a copy can be gotten from the agency.[72]

A public hearing on a proposed rule must be held if an agency receives a written request for a public hearing within fifteen days after the notice of text is published and the proposed text is not a changed version of proposed text previously published but not adopted.[73] A public hearing (or hearings) may be held on any rule. Most agencies that anticipate any significant public interest in a proposed rule will go ahead and schedule one or more hearings and publish their dates at the time the text of the proposed rule is published, to save time that would be lost by waiting for a public hearing request, then scheduling a hearing and separately publishing the date for the hearing. A public hearing cannot be held less than fifteen days after the date a notice of the hearing is published in the *North Carolina Register*.[74]

Notices of hearings and comment opportunities

Agency mailing lists

Agencies covered by the APA rule-making provisions must maintain a mailing list of persons who have requested notices of rule making. These persons must receive copies of all notices of text published, although an agency can separate rules by subject matter and send notices only to persons who ask for notices about a certain subject matter. An agency is allowed to charge an annual fee to each person on the mailing list to cover copying and mailing costs. [75]

There are very few statutory provisions governing the holding of public hearings. The form of hearings on rules has been flexible since the first North Carolina APA.[76] Trial-type hearings are not required; indeed, it is this and other commenters' view that oral hearings (speechmaking) probably are not required, though the law is unclear on this.[77] Oral hearings are often appropriate, though, and trial-type hearings may be called for in certain circumstances. As Professor Davis asserted:

Holding public hearings and receiving comments

> Any or all of the methods of party participation may be used
> for the formulation of one set of rules: an original draft may
> be prepared through consultation of the agency's staff with
> an advisory committee, then questionnaires or invitations for
> written comments may be sent to affected parties with or without
> submission of a tentative draft of the rules, then the tentative rules
> as modified may be discussed at a speechmaking type of hearing,
> and finally disputed issues of fact that emerge may be isolated for a
> trial-type hearing.[78]

The APA defines the term "hearing officer" in reference to contested cases (adjudication), not to rule making.[79] Agencies that have a significant volume of rule making are likely to have rules governing the holding of public hearings, and these agency-by-agency rules will likely be the supreme law on issues such as who can be a presiding officer, how comments are received at the hearing, and other details of how the hearing is conducted.[80] Basic constitutional provisions of fairness and informal due process should, of course, be followed, but beyond these minimal constitutional requirements—such as avoidance of discrimination and neutral application of whatever hearing rules are used—and any specific agency rules, there are few fixed legal requirements. The main fixed legal requirements concern the receipt and handling of comments. What follows this discussion of comments, then, are suggestions designed to make the hearing process work more efficiently and equitably, rather than legal requirements that must be followed.

When and how can comments be submitted?

The minimum period of time in which an APA covered rule-making agency must receive comments on a rule is sixty days, the period now required for comment after a notice of text.[81] This minimum time period assumes there is no public hearing; if there is a public hearing held after the minimum comment period has ended, the comments must be received until the public hearing.[82] By using the phrase "until the date of any public hearing," the statute appears to allow a comment period to be closed at the end of the day preceding a public hearing. But this would nullify an important purpose of the hearing and could frustrate the overall APA goal of ensuring that multiple points of view are considered in taking agency action.[83] So it is much better practice to keep a comment period open not just through any public hearing, but for a short time afterwards, to allow comments to be formulated, revised, and submitted following the often educational experience of the public hearing.

Who can be a presiding (or hearing) officer?

There are no statutory restrictions on who can be a presiding officer (hearing officer) at a public hearing on a proposed rule. Different agencies have approached the problem differently: some prefer staff who have been involved in the rule's development to preside, since they are most likely able to answer questions that could arise in the hearing and may be in the best position to understand and respond to comments. Others prefer those who will make the final decision for the agency on the rule to preside, or a representative of the final decision makers, on the theory that they are the ones who most need to hear the concerns raised and who also may be less wedded to a staff decision about wording or policy choice. Finally, some agencies may prefer having a third party preside, perhaps a neutral third party who has no direct stake in the proposed text or the final decision.

Conducting a hearing

The scope of issues that can arise in conducting a public hearing on a proposed rule is practically infinite. At many public hearings held by North Carolina agencies, few or no people show up to make comments and the major responsibility of the presiding officer is to turn the lights out and document the event. Yet at the next public hearing, there may be a serious need for security arrangements to keep the crowd orderly. Such is the diversity of rule making. Perhaps in recognition of this diversity, the law gives considerable discretion to hearing officers in making arrangements for and conducting hearings.

The main statutory requirement concerning the holding of public hearings, and the receipt of comments generally, is the requirement that "An agency must consider fully all written and oral comments received."[84] Anything the hearing officer does that prevents full consideration of all comments received, or anything the officer fails to do to ensure their full consideration, is problematic.

On the other hand, the holding of a public hearing is not a commitment by an agency to stay open for oral comments until everyone has said everything they wish. In other words, reasonable time limits on speakers are well within the discretion of the hearing officer, so long as there is no attempt to favor or disfavor any particular point of view being presented. When time limits are imposed on speakers, it is doubly useful for an agency to hold the record open for written comments for a few days after the public hearing, so that persons who did not get to speak or who did not finish their oral comments can submit something in writing and everyone can respond to points that were made orally.

Similarly, there is nothing illegal about a hearing officer limiting a speaker to comments that are germane to the rule-making proposal at hand, particularly if there are other speakers whose time is put at risk by undirected or misdirected rants. But this authority should be exercised very carefully, with a liberal allowance for what is deemed "germane." Otherwise, the agency may fail to consider fully all written and oral comments received."[85]

Could an agency require that an individual submit written comments, even if the individual also makes oral remarks? While this is good practice for commenters, to ensure correct transmission of their points, it appears inconsistent with the statute's requirement that an agency "consider fully all written and oral comments received."[86]

Adverse weather and other exigencies sometimes disrupt planned public hearings. The hearing officer has the discretion to cancel a public hearing. But if cancelled, it should normally be rescheduled following new publication of the date and place in the *North Carolina Register*, with the usual fifteen-day waiting period after publication of the new date. If a meeting is opened and then must be halted prematurely, the hearing officer has the option to continue the meeting until a later date. Notice of the new schedule should be given to all present and preferably posted at the location of the hearing, along with whatever other quick communication channels are open to the agency to contact persons interested in its rules.

Multiple hearings can be held on the same rule in order to give maximum possibility for comments that may vary across the state or a region of the state. If an agency plans to hold multiple hearings, and one or more of them is cancelled, there is no statutory requirement that each and every hearing be rescheduled. The only requirement is that the agency must hold "a" public hearing on a rule, if the other conditions requiring a hearing are met.[87]

Creating a record of a hearing

The record of a hearing is an important document and it is a principal responsibility of the hearing officer to ensure its preparation. It is statutorily required.[88] The statute requires the record to include

1. all written comments received;
2. a transcript or recording of any public hearing held on the rule; and
3. any written explanation made by the agency for adopting the rule.[89]

It would be difficult to consider fully all comments received if the presiding officer or other agency representative responsible for the hearing failed to make some record of who said what. The transcript or recording requirement ensures that this record is kept. It is useful to request that citizens sign an attendance sheet and write their names and contact information, and to include this in the record, but nothing in the statute compels this, though note that individual agency rules may. Audio- or videotaping can be helpful, but unless speakers identify themselves before speaking, there is no way to know who said what. Agencies that have a significant volume of rule making should have procedures in place to ensure that records of hearings are standard and complete enough for efficient review by final decision makers and later potential reviewers of the rule-making process.

Hearings without physical presence

One of the miracles of the modern age is the ability to collect and transmit audio and video signals over long distances and at different times. The APA has not yet taken notice of the possibilities for hearings held by telephone, over the Internet, or in whatever other ways information technology may ultimately permit. If an agency proposes to hold a hearing using information technology, such as by telephone or webcast, and no one who desires to comment objects, then there is nothing in the APA that prevents the agency from going forward in this fashion. It is likely that a day will come when technology makes the notice and comment process much better.

But that day is not yet at hand, at least legally, and if someone does object to the holding of a public hearing without the physical proximity of hearing officer and commenter, the law would seem to favor the objecting commenter. The APA statute on holding hearings speaks of the requirement to publish a notice of the "date, time and place of the public hearing."[90] "Date, time and place" describe real space, not cyberspace; the statutes contemplate an actual physical location and particular time for the hearing.

Responding to comments

An agency is not required to give responses to each and every comment received; it is only required to consider them fully. However, any person can request an explanation for a rule from an agency within thirty days after the rule is adopted. An agency that receives such a request must

- issue a concise written statement explaining why the agency adopted the rule,
- state the principal reasons for and against adopting the rule, and
- discuss why the agency rejected any arguments made or considerations urged against the adoption of the rule.[91]

Open meetings and public records issues

The full breadth of open meetings and public records issues as they relate to rule making is outside the scope of this book.[92] But agencies and interested parties should keep in mind that both the Open Meetings Law[93] and the Public Records Act[94] do apply fully to rule making. Under the Open Meetings Law, staff of an agency are entitled to have meetings among themselves to discuss the rule making without inviting the world to join them. Convene a majority of those responsible for a final decision on the rule, however, and they cannot discuss the proposed rule without affording advance notice under the law. Closed sessions are also strictly regulated under the Open Meetings Law. Public records in North Carolina, which include nearly everything written in any form by agency personnel in carrying out agency business, are legally open to be reviewed and copied. This includes pre-decisional memoranda and such things as drafts of rules, even when the final agency decision maker has not yet seen and approved them. There is no pre-decisional, deliberative exception to the North Carolina Public Records Act, as there is under the Federal Freedom of Information Act.[95]

Revising rules and the requirement to republish; the "moving target" problem

Some of the thorniest legal questions about rule making arise from what might be termed the "moving target" problem. In essence it is this: An agency publishes a proposed text of a rule, then seeks comment. If the agency is really fully considering the comment, as it is required to do, it may well identify parts of the proposed rule that need to be changed. But if it makes changes, how are the interested parties to be made aware of this? What if some changes made by the agency also change the position commenters might have on the rule? What if someone is affected adversely by the changes, even though they were not as affected by the original rule—can they be denied the time and opportunity to comment on the changes?

The statute seeks to solve this problem by creating a threshold level of significant change—a rule that "differs substantially from the text of a proposed rule" cannot be adopted without republishing the new text and going through the comment process again (not necessarily having another public hearing).[96] The statute gives a further gloss on "differs substantially":

> An adopted rule differs substantially from a proposed rule if it does one or more of the following:
>
> (1) Affects the interests of persons who, based on either the notice of rule making proceedings or the proposed text of the rule published in the *North Carolina Register*, could not reasonably have determined that the rule would affect their interests.
> (2) Addresses a subject matter or an issue that is not addressed in the proposed text of the rule.
> (3) Produces an effect that could not reasonably have been expected based on the proposed text of the rule.[97]

So, in the situation noted above, where a change in a rule produces some adverse effect for a person not previously affected by the rule, the statute is clear that the changed rule should be published for comment, starting the formal notice and comment process all over.

The pragmatic test of what "differs substantially" at this stage is whatever the Rules Review Commission says differs substantially. Thus, for close calls it may be worth discussing the matter with staff of the Rules Review Commission. A functional test of what "differs substantially" might ask whether anyone in the public would reasonably have been surprised or reasonably have relied to their detriment on the change not being made? It may help to consider a topical approach: If a proposed rule puts the public on notice that the topic of distance of wells from septic systems is at issue, then it is reasonable to suppose that the exact distances stated in the proposed rule might change. If the original proposed distance is twenty-five feet, and after comments this changes to twenty feet, a reasonable member of the public should not be surprised; they should not rely on the published distance as the final one.[98] Also, these tests all allow the format of a rule to change radically without rising to the level of a "substantially different" rule.

Once the comment period has closed, an agency—that is, the agency head or commission with the authority—may adopt a rule, as long as no more than twelve months have passed since the close of the comment period.[99]

Adoption of rules

Permanent rules: Review, legislative oversight, effectiveness, and judicial review

Adoption of the rule begins the long process of rules review, when the rule may be considered by the Office of State Budget and Management, the Governor's Office, the Rules Review Commission, and the legislature itself. Each of these institutions has some ability to be a gatekeeper for the rule; that is, to prevent its becoming effective. The legislature also has a committee charged with oversight of the entire rule-making process.

The Office of State Budget and Management reviews rules with fiscal notes—and rules that someone argues should have a fiscal note but do not. Their review is focused on the fiscal note and the corresponding fiscal implications of the rule. The type and criteria for budget review vary, depending on the type of fiscal impact.

Office of State Budget and Management

State fiscal impact. For rules that require the spending of state funds, the budget review must produce a "certification from the Director [of the Budget] that the funds that would be required by the proposed rule change are available."[100]

Local fiscal impact. Rules that affect the revenues or expenditures of a unit of local government must be circulated to the Office of the Governor, the Office of State Budget and Management, the Fiscal Research Division of the General Assembly, and the two local government associations, the League of Municipalities and Association of County Commissioners, along with an analysis of increased expenditures or revenues of local government. No particular type of review is required by statute.[101]

Substantial economic impact. Rules that are expected to have a substantial economic impact (at least $3 million in a twelve-month period) must have a fiscal note either prepared by or certified by the Office of State Budget and Management, unless the rule-making agency has requested the Office of State Budget and Management to prepare the fiscal note but, after ninety days, no note has been produced.[102]

When a rule does not have a fiscal note prepared for it, it does not ordinarily go for review by the Office of State Budget and Management. However, when the Rules Review Commission reviews the rule, it is free to ask the Office of State Budget and Management to determine whether the rule has a "substantial economic impact" as defined above. If the Rules Review Commission receives a written request for such a determination, it must ask the Office of State Budget and Management to make this call.[103] There is thus some risk of delay at the last minute for rules that are believed by someone to have substantial economic impact, but for which the agency does not want to prepare a fiscal note.

When the 1995 APA amendments were passed, greatly increasing the analytic requirements for rule making and adding the "substantial economic impact" review, there was much concern on the part of the agencies that they lacked the staff and expertise to do economic analysis on rules. The legislature imposed the analytic requirement anyway, and rather than fund positions in each agency to do economic analysis, it funded two positions for economists in the Office of State Budget and Management. These positions now are the gatekeepers for agency fiscal notes on rules.

Governor's Office

The governor, as the constitutionally appointed head of the executive branch, with responsibility to see that "the laws be faithfully executed,"[104] has in some sense the ultimate say on whether rules will proceed. However, as in many states, North Carolina's structure of government is much more fractured than its apparently clear, three-branch constitutional structure would indicate. As noted above, there are some departments in the executive branch with agency heads appointed by and serving at the pleasure of the governor. These, his cabinet agencies, have a clear line of responsibility and accountability to the governor and thus could have their rules "vetoed" by the governor. The governor could issue and, at times, has issued executive orders directing how and when rules arising from these cabinet agencies will be reviewed by the Governor's Office. However, even within these agencies, there are separate rule-making bodies, notably commissions of persons appointed partly by the governor and partly by the legislative leadership. It is by no means constitutionally clear that the governor could veto a rule-making decision of these bodies. Then there are the separately elected agency heads who form the Council of State over which the governor has little formal legal authority. Finally, there is a class of agencies, such as the

Office of Administrative Hearings and the Rules Review Commission themselves, that are nominally located in the executive branch, but that have agency heads appointed by non–executive branch personnel. So the governor's role in executive agency rule making is not as clear as it might seem at first.

The legislature has inserted the Governor's Office into one particular class of rule review: rules that affect the expenditures or revenues of a unit of local government. The APA requires that at least thirty days before an agency publishes the proposed text of a permanent rule that would have such an effect, the agency (this would mean any agency, not just those in the governor's cabinet) must submit the text of the rule, a short explanation, and the local fiscal note to the governor for preliminary review.[105] The statute directs the governor to consider the agency's reason for the proposed change, any unanticipated effects of the change on local government, and the potential costs of the proposed change weighed against the potential risks to the public of not taking the proposed change.[106] This review requirement was added as part of the 1995 amendments, but it represented a codification of an executive order already then in place.

The Rules Review Commission is a state agency with ten part-time commissioners appointed by the legislative leadership, along with a small, full-time staff.[107] It meets monthly, normally on the third Thursday of each month, and requires the presence of six commissioners for a quorum. The job of the Rules Review Commission is to review every temporary and permanent rule proposed in North Carolina.[108] The Rules Review Commission can "veto" a rule (stop it from becoming effective) if it finds that the rule fails one of the following criteria:

Rules Review Commission

(1) It is within the authority delegated to the agency by the General Assembly.
(2) It is clear and unambiguous.
(3) It is reasonably necessary to implement or interpret an enactment of the General Assembly, or of Congress, or a regulation of a federal agency. The Commission shall consider the cumulative effect of all rules adopted by the agency related to the specific purpose for which the rule is proposed.
(4) It was adopted in accordance with Part 2 of [Article 2A of the APA].[109]

With the 2003 APA changes, the Rules Review Commission was also directed to "not consider questions relating to the quality or efficacy of the rule," but rather to "restrict its review to determination of the standards set forth [above]."[110]

If the commission objects to a rule, it must send a written statement explaining the objection to the agency. The agency then may attempt to satisfy the commission's objection and resubmit the revised rule for further review, or it may refuse, in which case the rule does not become effective.[111] The scope of the Rules Review Commission's review includes the entire rule, not just portions that may be proposed for change by an agency.[112] This means that an agency that proposes changes in one part of a long-standing rule may find itself having to defend the authority, clarity, or burdensomeness of the original rule, and may even see the original rule struck by the Rules Review Commission. The commission staff may also send a "Request for a Technical Change" to agency rule-making staff if there are typographical or simple grammatical or wording problems with the proposed rule. These technical requests can be responded to immediately and returned before the commission meeting in order to keep a rule on track for review. The commission staff normally give APA coordinators in the agency advance notice of the staff opinion about a set of proposed rules. These opinions are important, although not determinative, predictors of the full commission's action.

The review process by the Rules Review Commission is normally straightforward, but can present some subtleties. There are several time limits on the process of rules review. The Rules Review Commission must review a permanent rule submitted to it on or before the twentieth of the month by the last day of the next month; rules that come in after the twentieth of a month must be reviewed by the last day of the second subsequent month.[113] After an objection by the Rules Review Commission, an agency must decide whether to revise the rule and attempt to satisfy the objection, or not, within thirty days after receiving the objection (for an agency other than a board or commission) or within ten days after the board or commission's next meeting (for a board or commission, if the ten-day period is longer than the thirty-day deadline).[114] While the agency is making this decision, the rule remains nominally under review by the Rules Review Commission.[115]

For temporary rules, the Rules Review Commission is to review the proposed rule within fifteen business days after receiving it, and the statute allows this expedited review to take place by a staff attorney and the Rules Review Commission working through a panel of at least three members of the commission.[116] On approval of the temporary rules, the commission or its designee has two business days to deliver the rule to the codifier of rules, who then must enter it into the *North Carolina Administrative Code* on the sixth business day after receipt. If the Rules Review Commission disapproves the temporary rule, and the agency attempts to satisfy the objection with new information, the Rules Review Commission or designee has five business days to respond.[117]

After an objection, the question has arisen as to who has authority to reconsider and make changes to the proposed rules. The statute simply says it is "the agency that adopted the rule."[118] When this is a board or commission, the issue is whether the staff that serves that board or commission can negotiate and make wording changes that satisfy the Rules Review Commission objections or whether this action must be taken by the full board or commission. This is a question of delegation within the agency. The agency head, whether a department secretary or a commission, should make clear in its own procedures the extent to which staff are permitted to make changes to satisfy the Rules Review Commission without coming back to the agency head for review of the changes. Each APA coordinator should review the rules for rule making and delegations in place for that coordinator's agencies to make sure the extent of this power is understood. In 2004 the legislature expressly authorized agencies to change the effective dates of rules so that all parts of a "rule package" can move through later steps of the rule making process together. This can be important when RRC objections affect only part of a series of rules that are designed to work together.[119]

The constitutional legitimacy of the Rules Review Commission has been attacked on several occasions.[120] The main lines of attack usually center around some variant of the question whether the Commission is an impermissible foray by the legislative branch into the business of the executive branch. To date, none of these attacks has reached a resolution by the courts.

Codifier of rules/Office of Administrative Hearings

Once a temporary or permanent rule has been approved by the Rules Review Commission, it is filed with the Office of Administrative Hearings for inclusion in the *North Carolina Administrative Code*. The Office of Administrative Hearings is the office of the codifier of rules in North Carolina. As the agency in charge of both the *North Carolina Register* (publication of notices of the text of proposed rules) and the *North Carolina Administrative Code* (the official published version of North Carolina administrative rules), as well as the locus of decisions about the propriety of emergency rules, the Office of Administrative Hearings is a very important source of information and advice about rule making in North Carolina. APA coordinators should be familiar with the office's rules governing rule making, which are published at 26 N.C.A.C. 2C.

The General Assembly

With the 1995 and 2003 amendments to North Carolina's APA, certain "controversial" permanent rules do not become effective until (at the earliest) the thirty-first legislative day of the next regular session of the General Assembly that is begun at least twenty-five days after the rule is approved by the Rules Review Commission.[121] *Controversial rules* are those about which the Rules Review Commission receives written objections from ten or more persons "clearly requesting review by the legislature."[122] Such rules have delayed effective dates. The delay gives a chance for any legislator to introduce a bill to "kill" the rule, that is, to prevent the rule from ever becoming effective. The "kill bill" must "specifically disapprove" the rule by giving its citation in the *North Carolina Administrative Code* and stating that it is disapproved.[123] If a "kill bill" is introduced before the thirty-first legislative day, then the effective date of the rule must await final legislative disposition of the bill. If the bill passes, the rule never becomes effective. If the bill fails by adverse final action, the rule becomes effective the day the bill is defeated. Final action on bills that are not destined to pass often never occurs, meaning that the effective date of the rule may well be the day the legislative session adjourns.

The North Carolina APA does permit the governor, by executive order, to make effective a permanent rule that has been approved by the Rules Review Commission before it passes the legislative gauntlet.[124] To make a rule effective, the executive order must find that "it is necessary that the rule become effective in order to protect public health, safety, or welfare." Furthermore, a rule made effective in this manner remains in effect unless it is specifically disapproved by a bill passed by the General Assembly.[125] Rules made effective by executive order must be specially indicated in the *North Carolina Administrative Code.* This provision was added with the 1995 amendments as a "safety valve" to allow rules to be made effective earlier than the thirty-first day of the next general session, because that effective date requirement can postpone the effectiveness of an approved rule for a long time—over a year. For example, a rule that the Rules Review Commission approves in January of a year in which the long session of the General Assembly convenes in January might not become effective, absent executive order, until July of the following year, a month after the next regular session (the short session) of the legislature begins. Despite this concern, in its first nine years, the executive order exception was rarely, if ever, used.

An agency rule that is delayed by objections may also be put into effect as a temporary rule, pursuant to G.S. 150B-21.3(b2), if the rule would have met the threshold requirements for a temporary rule at G.S. 150B-21.1(a).

Joint Legislative Oversight Committee

Another new mechanism for oversight of rule making was added by the 1995 APA amendments: the Joint Legislative Administrative Procedure Oversight Committee.[126] This is a sixteen-member bicameral committee of the legislature with the general power and duty to review rules objected to by the Rules Review Commission and in other ways to provide oversight for the rule-making process. To date, the Legislative Oversight Committee's primary focus has been review of proposed rules that members of the committee believed might be unduly burdensome, inefficient or unfair. In other words, the committee has become a forum for legislative inquiry into particular rules about which legislators have heard complaints. It is important to note that the Legislative Oversight Committee does not itself approve or veto rules. It simply receives reports from the Rules Review Commission, or undertakes investigations on its own, and as a result of those reports and investigations, it may recommend legislation to the full General Assembly.

Judicial review of rules in North Carolina generally takes place only when a rule is applied to a particular person,[127] except for challenges to vetoes by the Rules Review Commission[128] and challenges to temporary and emergency rules.[129] The fact of limited judicial review of rule making alone creates major differences in the way rule making is done and perceived in North Carolina, as compared to the federal government. Many, if not most, controversial rules in the federal system are challenged when they are promulgated, even before they are applied, and the federal courts have shown some willingness to inquire into the process and merits of the new rules themselves. In contrast, "Entry of a rule in the North Carolina Administrative Code after review by the [Rules Review] Commission creates a rebuttable presumption that the rule was adopted in accordance with [the APA rule-making provisions.]"[130] This means that once codified, a North Carolina rule is difficult to challenge other than in a challenge to the circumstances or fairness of its application to a particular person. There are at least two procedural mechanisms for getting a court to review a rule directly (rather than reviewing its application in a particular case): a declaratory judgment action in superior court and a rule-making petition (discussed below). But rule making is a quasi-legislative activity, so the merits of the agency's policy choices in any given rule are unlikely to be disturbed by a court, absent some constitutional problem.

The ancient writ of certiorari remains a theoretical avenue for judicial review of any administrative action: "Courts have inherent authority to review the actions of any administrative agency whenever such actions affect personal or property rights, upon a prima facie showing, by petition for certiorari, that such agency has acted arbitrarily, capriciously or in disregard of law."[131] But certiorari is a discretionary writ.[132] North Carolina courts generally have stuck to the view that "where a statute provides an orderly procedure for appeal, certiorari will not lie as a substitute for an appeal, but is proper only when the aggrieved party cannot perfect his appeal within the time limited and such inability is not due to any fault on his part."[133] In the rule-making context, this will generally mean that persons opposed to a rule or the form a rule ultimately takes will be best served (at least procedurally) by awaiting application of the rule to challenge it before a court.

There is an administrative procedure for getting judicial review of a rule in North Carolina. One can petition the rule-making agency to adopt a rule preferred by the petitioner and then seek judicial review of the agency's refusal to adopt that rule.[134] An agency must grant or deny a rule-making petition within thirty days after it is submitted, unless the agency is a board or commission, in which case it must grant or deny the petition within 120 days after it is submitted. Once a petition is denied, judicial review is immediately available.[135] So it is conceivable that a person who dislikes a choice made by an agency in the course of an agency's rule-making proceedings could get before a judge with alternative language before the agency's rule is effective. The process would involve a petition to the agency to adopt an alternative rule and soliciting nine other persons to request a delayed effective date for the agency's rule. However, there would be little likelihood of success for such a petitioner unless the agency's rule departed significantly from some standard, criteria, or policy choice that the legislature had clearly imposed on the agency.

The North Carolina APA does provide a direct route for challenging temporary and emergency rules. A "person aggrieved" by a temporary or emergency rule is authorized to file a declaratory judgment action in Wake County Superior Court, and the court is directed to "determine whether the agency's written statement of findings of need for the rule meets the criteria listed [for temporary or emergency rule making, respectively] and whether the rule meets the standards in G.S. 150B-21.9 [the Rules Review Commission review standards]. . . ."[136] By implication, the quality and efficacy of the rule are not justiciable issues in the declaratory judgment action.[137] Further, the court is precluded from granting an ex parte temporary restraining order.[138]

Prior to 1995, the North Carolina APA authorized declaratory judgment actions when the Rules Review Commission objected to an agency's authority to make the rule.[139] This statute became superfluous and was repealed when the Rules Review Commission got "veto" power; rules can no longer be made effective over the commission's objection. The last set of rules to be challenged under this provision were wetlands rules from the Department of Environment and Natural Resources (DENR).[140] The commission objected to the authority of DENR to make the rules; DENR published the rules over the commission's objection; and a group of business and developer associations challenged the rules in Superior Court. The Superior Court and Court of Appeals upheld the authority of DENR.[141]

It is ironic that two of the most difficult rule-making review processes for the State of North Carolina have been environmental rules, for regulation of development in wetlands and for regulation of stormwater. The irony comes from the oft-repeated claim of the main legislative proponent for the 1995 rule-making changes, former Sen. J.K. Sherron, a real estate broker and developer in Raleigh, that his proposed rule-making revisions were not intended to target environmental rules. The period of greatest complexity and length in rule making in North Carolina was bracketed by environmental rules: wetlands in 1995 and stormwater in 2003. Perhaps the 2003 reforms, with their explicit attempt to separate out "controversial" rules, will finally achieve a stable balance between efficiency and fairness in rule making.

Figure 2-3 is a flow chart of the permanent rule-making process prepared by the Office of Administrative Hearings shortly after passage of the 2003 APA reforms.

Figure 2-3.
Permanent Rule-Making Process

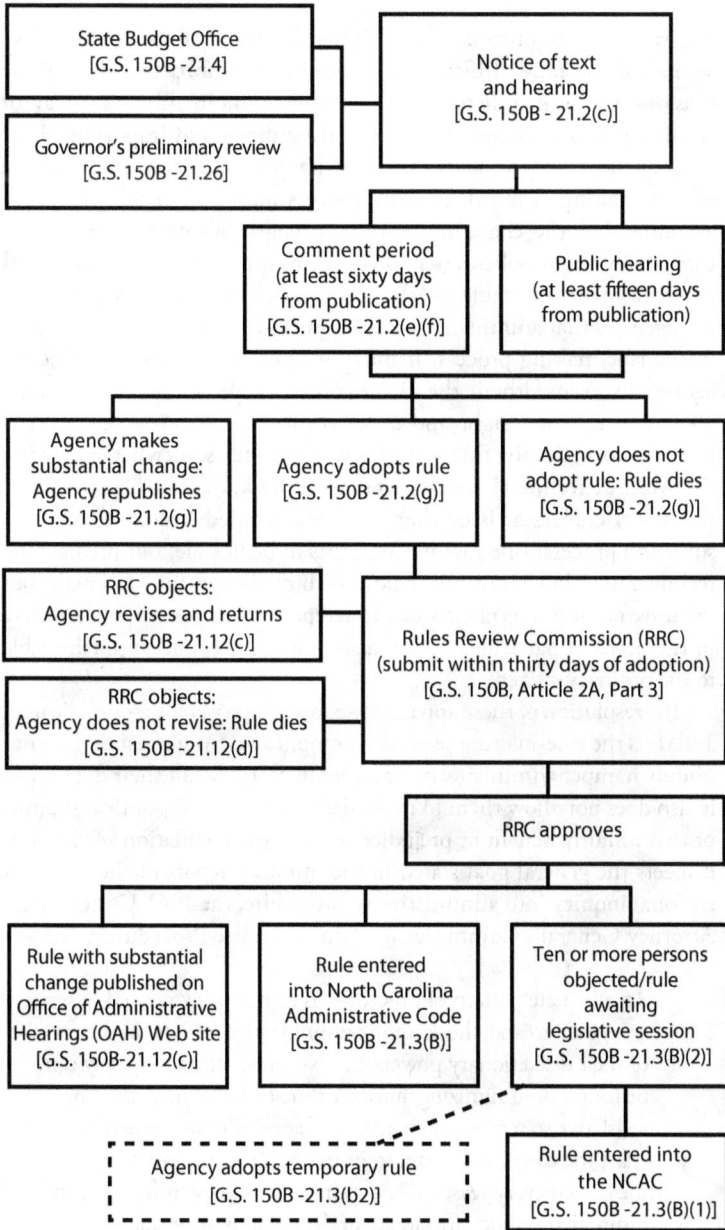

```
┌─────────────────────────┐
│ State Budget Office      │          ┌──────────────────────┐
│ [G.S. 150B -21.4]        │          │ Notice of text       │
└─────────────────────────┘          │ and hearing          │
                                      │ [G.S. 150B - 21.2(c)]│
┌─────────────────────────┐          └──────────────────────┘
│ Governor's preliminary  │
│ review                   │
│ [G.S. 150B -21.26]       │
└─────────────────────────┘
```

| Comment period (at least sixty days from publication) [G.S. 150B -21.2(e)(f)] | Public hearing (at least fifteen days from publication) |

| Agency makes substantial change: Agency republishes [G.S. 150B -21.2(g)] | Agency adopts rule [G.S. 150B -21.2(g)] | Agency does not adopt rule: Rule dies [G.S. 150B -21.2(g)] |

| RRC objects: Agency revises and returns [G.S. 150B -21.12(c)] | Rules Review Commission (RRC) (submit within thirty days of adoption) [G.S. 150B, Article 2A, Part 3] |
| RRC objects: Agency does not revise: Rule dies [G.S. 150B -21.12(d)] | |

RRC approves

| Rule with substantial change published on Office of Administrative Hearings (OAH) Web site [G.S. 150B-21.12(c)] | Rule entered into North Carolina Administrative Code [G.S. 150B -21.3(B)] | Ten or more persons objected/rule awaiting legislative session [G.S. 150B -21.3(B)(2)] |

| Agency adopts temporary rule [G.S. 150B -21.3(b2)] | Rule entered into the NCAC [G.S. 150B -21.3(B)(1)] |

Note: This document is based on a document prepared by the Office of Administrative Hearings as a public service and is not to be deemed binding or controlling. (09/17/03)

Why is the process of rule making so complicated?

The rule-making process is complicated because it attempts to resolve several of the most difficult tensions in American democracy. These tensions are deep, inherent, and dynamic. Rule making is a way of turning policy into law. It is inherently difficult and important. Real consequences for people's wealth and happiness turn on the outcome of rule making. The rule-making process must be flexible enough to accommodate the changing political strength of interest groups that care deeply about policies that affect them. It must be stable enough to be somewhat predictable, so that persons affected by rules (including the agencies that administer them) know how to follow and participate in the rule-making process. It must be open enough to be politically legitimate, even without the direct control of elected officials. It must allow for some oversight and a degree of control by elected officials in order to maintain this legitimacy, while still somewhat insulating the work of technical experts who typically know much more about the policy choices at issue than do any interested elected officials. In sum, as a process, rule making attempts to be flexible, but predictable; technocratic, but political; efficient, but thoughtful; rational, but inclusive of the points of view of affected persons; consistent, but sensitive to the needs of particular policy areas; and precise, but comprehensible to the ordinary citizen.

The resolution of these apparently contradictory goals is complicated, and thus the rule-making process is complicated. At its best, it does not unduly hamper administrative agencies in carrying out their duties, but it also does not allow them to make decisions that lack political support or that unfairly benefit or prejudice parts of the population. At its best, it meets the general goal stated in the minority report of the very first national inquiry into administrative procedure, the 1941 United States Attorney General's Committee on Administrative Procedure:

> An adequate pattern of procedure is imperatively needed to serve as a guide to and check upon administrative officials in the exercise of their discretionary powers. . . . No more satisfactory way can be found of minimizing abuses, or the fear of abuses, than by legislative statement of standards of administrative procedure to chart the course of action, to insure publicity of process, to give the citizen every reasonable opportunity to present his case, and to insure that public officials act under circumstances calculated to produce a fair and prompt result.[142]

A brief history of rule making in North Carolina

In the first hundred years of state administrative law in the United States, North Carolina has always been among the leading states in adopting new approaches to administrative procedure, including rule making. In 1939, North Carolina passed a Uniform Licensing Act,[143] placing the state in the group of eight states that passed administrative procedure laws during the first period of United States administrative law reform.[144] This first period began with the reaction, led by the American Bar Association, to the rise of federal agencies created to deal with the problems of the Great Depression.[145]

The end of World War II brought renewed attention to administrative law, and the nation passed the Administrative Procedures Act in 1946. In the same year, the National Conference of Commissioners on Uniform State Laws formally approved its first model state administrative procedures act and recommended its adoption to the states.[146] North Carolina was one of twelve states to pass legislation based in part on the model act.[147]

Former Article 18 of G.S. 143 (G.S. 143-195 and -196) required that administrative rules (the term was undefined) previously adopted were effective until June 1, 1943, but thereafter were effective only after filing with the secretary of state:

> On or before the first day of June of 1943, each agency of the State of North Carolina created by statute and authorized to exercise regulatory, administrative or semi-judicial functions, shall file with the Secretary of State a complete copy of all general administrative rules and regulations or rules of practices and procedure, formulated or adopted by the agency for the performance of its functions or for the exercise of its authority and shall thereafter, immediately upon the adoption of any new general administrative rule or regulation or rule of practice and procedure, or the formulation or adoption of any amendment to any general administrative rule or regulation or rule of practice and procedure, file a copy of the same with the Secretary of State: Provided that nothing contained in this article shall require any State agency to file in the office of the Secretary of State any rate, service or tariff schedule or order or any administrative rule or regulation referring to any such rate, service or tariff schedule.[148]

The General Assembly in 1953 passed an act entitled "Judicial Review of Decisions of Certain Administrative Agencies."[149] The Judicial Review Act provided that "Any person who is aggrieved by a final administrative decision, and who has exhausted all administrative remedies made available to him by statute or agency rule, is entitled to judicial review of such decision under this article, unless adequate procedure for judicial review is provided by some other statute." [150]

A report prepared by the Institute of Government for the Committee on Administrative Law of the North Carolina Bar Association in 1960 reviewed the then-current ways that administrative rules were published in several other states. [151] As noted, at that time, filing of most administrative rules with the secretary of state was required, and where the rules had the force and effect of criminal law, [152] filing was also required with clerks of superior court. The report noted a major flaw with that filing system, which was that "officials with whom rules and regulations are filed have not maintained them in a usable collection." They simply went into a filing cabinet. [153]

The Model State Administrative Procedures Act was revised in 1961. This 1961 model act was the basis for much of North Carolina's first comprehensive administrative procedures act, passed in 1974. [154] North Carolina thus joined the more than half the states in the country that have adopted general and comprehensive administrative procedures based in whole or in part on the 1946 or 1961 model state administrative procedures act. [155]

The state auditor's office conducted a survey and published findings in 1976 on the costs and benefits of the new APA. [156] An appendix to the report contains an interesting collection of letters from agencies, both those excluded and those covered by the new APA, with their agency head's impressions of costs and benefits. The survey instrument went to eighteen agencies; eleven reported that their administrative rules were available to the public prior to passage of the APA. Six reported that "some" of their rules were available, and one reported that its rules were not available prior to the APA. [157]

The model state administrative procedures act was again revised in 1981. North Carolina followed in 1985 with major changes to its administrative procedures act, although the changes were driven less by the presence of a revised model act than by general awareness of weaknesses in the first North Carolina administrative procedures act. In 1985, while the legislature considered the changes in the APA that produced the Office of Administrative Hearings, the North Carolina Center for Public Policy Research published a report on the APA. [158] The survey has a very good timeline summary of APA history in North Carolina. [159] Like the auditor in 1976, the center surveyed state agencies (ninety-two persons, with a response from sixty-five). Among other findings, APA coordinators reported that ten or fewer persons attended about half the rule-making hearings. [160] The people commenting on proposed rules were believed by survey respondents to represent overwhelmingly business interests and regulated persons. Public interest groups were a distant third and interested citizens fifth.[161] Rules were still not published as of the time of this survey. They were available on microfiche.

Thirty-three percent of survey respondents said the APA process was too time consuming; this ranked as the greatest weakness of the APA rule-making provisions, according to this survey.[162] This is ironically amusing, given how much longer it takes today.[163]

Notes

1. The Institute of Government at the University of North Carolina at Chapel Hill publishes these summaries on the Internet. Check the Institute's Legislative Summary at http://sog.unc.edu/pubs/nclegis/index.html for summaries of recent changes.

2. *E.g.*, Whittington v. N.C. Dep't of Human Resources, 100 N.C. App. 603 (1990) (rules on state-funded abortions).

3. *See* Conservation Council v. Haste, 102 N.C. App. 411 (1991) [relationship of Coastal Area Management Act notice and comment provisions to Administrative Procedure Act (APA) temporary rule comment provisions].

4. Temporary rule numbers:

Year	Number
1992/93	212
93/94	251
94/95	239
95/96	211
96/97	208
98/99	360
99/2000	769
00/01	436
01/02	777
02/03	663
03/04	74
04/05	39

Note: Based on data supplied by the Office of Administrative Hearings, on file with the author.

5. Chapter 150B, Section 21.1A(a), of the North Carolina General Statutes (hereinafter G.S.).

6. G.S. 150B-21.1A(a).

7. G.S. 150B-21.1A(a).

8. G.S. 150B-21.1A(b).

9. G.S. 150B-21.1A(a).

10. G.S. 150B-21.1A(b).

11. G.S. 150B-21.3(a).

12. G.S. 150B-21.1A(e).

13. G.S. 150B-21.1A(b).

14. G.S. 150B-21.1A(d).

15. G.S. 150B-21.1 (d).

16. "Emergency rules" (the original APA term, before "temporary rules")

were good for only one period. That period used to be 120 days, as in the 1961 Model State APA. The 1961 Model State APA explicitly allowed one extension of duration to be filled in by the state. *See* National Conference of Commissioners on Uniform State Laws § 3 (b), Uniform Law Commissioners' Revised Model State Administrative Procedure Act (Chicago, Ill.: 1961). Professor Charles Daye noted that renewals under the original North Carolina APA were clearly meant to be for only one 120-day period. CHARLES E. DAYE, *North Carolina's New Administrative Procedure Act: An Interpretive Analysis*, 53 N.C. L. REV. at 863 (1975) (Daye 1975).

17. G.S. 150B-21.1A(d).

18. G.S. 150B-21.1(a). There are also no less than seven specific grounds for temporary rule making that were granted to specific agencies in the 1990s and early 2000s, including exceptions for the State Medical Facilities Plan, the Wildlife Resources Commission, the secretary of state, the commissioner of insurance, the chief information officer, the State Board of Elections, and the Department of Health and Human Services. See the discussion of special exceptions to the temporary rule making process, *infra.*

19. http://ncrules.state.nc.us/proposedtempora_/default.htm.

20. G.S. 150B-21.1(a3).

21. G.S. 150B-21.1(a3).

22. G.S. 150B-21.1(b).

23. G.S. 150B-21.1(b). The Rules Review Commission (RRC) was given this gatekeeper role for temporary rules by the 2003 changes to the APA.

24. G.S. 150B-21.1(b).

25. G.S. 150B-21.9.

26. Before this 2003 legislative definition, the Office of Administrative Hearings (OAH) had promulgated a rule that defined "'recent Act' or 'recent change' [as] an act or change that was effective no more than 180 days before the submission date of the temporary rule to OAH." 26 NCAC. 02C.0102 (now repealed).

27. For such exceptions, see, e.g., S. L. 1998-221, sec. 1.12 (extending the time for temporary rules to be drafted for the Neuse River Nutrient Sensitive Waters Strategy and for revisions to the Erosion and Sediment Control program).

28. G.S. 150B-21.1(b).

29. G.S. 150B-21.1(b).

30. G.S. 150B-21.3(a).

31. G.S. 150B-21.1(e). Prior to 2002, agencies were also required to publish a "notice of rule making" giving advance notice of the subject matter of upcoming rules. Publication of the temporary rule in the *North Carolina Register* satisfied this requirement. Such advance notices are no longer required.

32. G.S. 150B-21.1(b).

33. G.S. 150B-21.1(d).

34. G.S. 150B-21.1 (d).

35. "Emergency rules" (the original APA term, before "temporary rules") were good for only one period. That period used to be 120 days, as in the 1961 Model State APA. The 1961 Model State APA explicitly allowed one extension of duration to be filled in by the state. *See* National Conference of Commissioners on Uniform State Laws § 3 (b), Uniform Law Commissioners'

Revised Model State Administrative Procedure Act (Chicago, Ill.: 1961). Prof. Daye noted that renewals under the original North Carolina APA were clearly meant to be for only one 120-day period. (Daye 1975, at 863.)

36. G.S. 150B-21.1(d).

37. G.S. 150B-21.1(a)(7).

38. *E.g.*, G.S. 113-292(c1).

39. G.S. 113-221.1.

40. G.S. 150B-21.1(a2).

41. G.S. 150B-21.1(a3).

42. G.S. 150B-21.1(a4).

43. G.S. 150B-21.1(a5).

44. The APA permanent rule process as it existed from 1995, when the Rules Review Commission "veto" provisions were added, until 2003 could easily take as long as eighteen months for any rule to be created or changed. The APA as originally adopted in North Carolina required at least ten days' notice before a hearing was held and at least twenty days before the adoption, amendment, or repeal of a rule. G.S. § 150A-12(a) (repealed). Prof. Daye seemed worried even in 1975 that the original requirement of having to hold a public hearing with oral speeches allowed would be enough to deter agencies from using rule making as fully as they should. (Daye 1975, at 860.) This worry is still present today, given the many additional procedural hurdles that must be cleared before a rule is finalized.

45. G.S. 150B-21.5(a).

46. G.S. 150B-21.5(b).

47. G.S. 150B-21.5(c).

48. G.S. 150B-21.20.

49. For example, when the Department of Health and Human Services was reorganized in 1997 to bring public health functions more fully under the department, the legislature expressly authorized a corresponding reorganization of its rules.

50. G.S. 150B-21(a), (c).

51. G.S. 150B-21(a).

52. G.S. 150B-21.6.

53. G.S. 150B-21.6.

54. G.S. 150B-21.6.

55. G.S. 150B-21.19(3); 26 NCAC 02C.0106.

56. *Cf.* G.S. 150B-21.20(2), (5) (giving the codifier of rules the power to revise headings and catchlines and "make other changes in arrangement or in form that do not change the substance of the rule . . . ").

57. 26 NCAC 02C.0108.

58. The Office of Administrative Hearings is at 919-733-2691 at the time of publication of this book.

59. For a survey of state-based regulatory reforms and a discussion of the N.C. Department of Environment, Health and Natural Resources' response to the 1995 amendments, see Richard Whisnant and Diane Cherry, *Economic Analysis of Rules: Devolution, Evolution and Realism*, 31 Wake Forest L. Rev. 693 (Fall 1996).

60. G.S. 150B-21.4(a).

61. G.S. 150B-21.4(b); 150B-21.26.

62. G.S. 150B –21.4(b)

63. G.S. 150B-21.27.

64. G.S. 150B-21.4(b1). This threshold amount was originally set at $5 million in the 1995 APA reform bill but was lowered to $3 million in 2003.

65. G.S. 150B-21.4(b1).

66. G.S. 150B-21.4(b2).

67. G.S. 150B-21.4(c).

68. G.S. 150B-21(f).

69. See delegation discussion on pages 12 to 15 of this book.

70. G.S. 150B-21.2(a)(1). Between 1995 and 2003, agencies were required to publish a preliminary document, the "notice of rule-making proceedings," or a regulatory agenda similar to the forecast of rule making required at the federal level. A notice of rule-making proceedings had to appear sixty days before publication of a notice of text. The notice of rule-making proceedings included four elements: (1) the subject matter of the rule making; (2) a short explanation of the reasons for the rule making; (3) the legal authority for the rule making; and (4) a contact person for questions or comments about the rule making. This advance notice of rule making was apparently not considered useful by interested parties.

71. G.S. 150B-21.2(d).

72. G.S. 150B-21.2(c).

73. G.S. 150B-21.2(e).

74. G.S. 150B-21.2(e).

75. G.S. 150B-21.2(d).

76. *See* DAYE 1975, at 857–59.

77. *See* DAYE 1975, at 858–59.

78. KENNETH C. DAVIS, TREATISE (1958) § 6.01.

79. G.S. 150B-2(2b). This definition is apparently an artifact from the days before the creation of central panel, full-time administrative law judges. The provisions of Article 3A of the APA, which govern contested case hearings held outside of the central panel, refer to a "presiding officer" rather than a "hearing officer." G.S. 150B-40.

80. *See, e.g.,* 15A NCAC 2I.0101–.0105 (rules for public hearings of the Environmental Management Commission).

81. G.S. 150B-21.2(f). Between 1995 and 2003 this period was 90 days: 60 days after the preliminary notice of rule-making proceedings and 30 days after the notice of text. For a rule that required a fiscal note because of substantial economic impact, the comment period after the text was published was at least 60 days, making the minimum overall time in which to receive comments on a rule with substantial economic impact 120 days under the pre-2003 process.

82. G.S. 150B-21.2(f).

83. *Cf.* G.S. 150B-1 ("the procedures ensure that the functions of rule making . . . are not all performed by the same person in the administrative process").

84. G.S. 150B-21.2(f).

85. G.S. 150B-21.2(f) *(emphasis added)*.

86. G.S. 150B-21.2(f) *(emphasis added)*.

87. G.S. 150B-21.2(e).

88. G.S. 150B-21.2(i)

89. G.S. 150B-21.2(i)

90. G.S. 150B-21.2(e).

91. G.S. 150B-21.2(h).

92. For good coverage of these topics under North Carolina law, see DAVID M. LAWRENCE, PUBLIC RECORDS LAW FOR NORTH CAROLINA LOCAL GOVERNMENTS (Chapel Hill: Institute of Government, 1997); DAVID M. LAWRENCE, OPEN MEETINGS AND LOCAL GOVERNMENTS IN NORTH CAROLINA: SOME QUESTIONS AND ANSWERS (Chapel Hill: Institute of Government, 4th ed., 1994).

93. G.S. 143-318.9 to -318.18.

94. G.S. 132-1 to 132.10.

95. *See, e.g.,* News and Observer Publishing Co., Inc. v. Poole, 330 N.C. 465, 412 S.E.2d 7 (1992) and discussion in LAWRENCE, PUBLIC RECORDS, *supra* note 166 at 11–13.

96. G.S. 150B-21.2(g)

97. G.S. 150B-21.2(g).

98. This example comes from an actual rule of the Environmental Management Commission, 15A NCAC 2C.107 (Oct. 12, 2000), approved by the Rules Review Commission but later revised by the legislature. *See* S.L. 2001-113 (H 609).

99. G.S. 150B-21.2(g).

100. G.S. 150B-21.4(a).

101. G.S. 150B-21.4(b).

102. G.S. 150B-21.4(b1).

103. G.S. 150B-21.9.

104. N.C. Const. art. III, § 5, cl. 4.

105. G.S. 150B-21.26.

106. G.S. 150B-21.26.

107. *See* G.S. 143B-30.1. The Commission was created by the General Assembly in 1986, and its powers were significantly broadened in 1995. In 2004 the Rules Review Commission staff was placed under the supervision of the Office of Administrative Hearings by Section 22A of the appropriations act, S.L. 2004-124.

108. Review of temporary rules was added in 2003.

109. G.S. 150B-21.9. The "reasonably necessary" language has been tinkered with several times in attempts to explain just what it means. Immediately prior to the 2003 changes, it read: "It is reasonably necessary to fulfill a duty delegated to the agency by the General Assembly, when considered in light of the cumulative effect of all rules adopted by the agency related to the specific purpose for which the rule is proposed and the legislative intent of the General Assembly in delegating the duty."

110. G.S. 150B-21.9.

111. G.S. 150B-21.12.

112. G.S. 150B-21.8(c).

113. G.S. 150B-21.9(b). The commission will accept rules filed by the close of business of the first business day after the twentieth day of the month if the twentieth day is a holiday.

114. G.S. 150B-21.12(b). The agency must consider whether any changes it makes constitute "substantial changes." *See* G.S. 150B-21.12(c) and *supra* at 46. In *Environmental Management Commission v. Rules Review Commission,*

4 CVS 3157 (Wake County Superior Court, June 15, 2005), the court rejected a claim that the agency had made a substantial change in Phase II Stormwater rules that triggered new notice and comment requirements.

115. G.S. 150B-21.12(d).

116. G.S. 150B-21.1(b).

117. G.S. 150B-21.1(b).

118. G.S. 150B-21.1(b) (temporary rule), 150B-21.12(a) (permanent rule).

119. S.L. 2004-156.

120. *See, e.g.*, Associated Press—Raleigh, *Group Sues State Panel Over Rules* (March 9, 2004), journalnow.com (regarding decision of Southern Environmental Law Center to file suit over the Phase II Stormwater Rules); Bruce Henderson, *Tug-of-War Under Way on Water Rules*, CHARLOTTE OBSERVER, February 13, 2004 (noting vote of Environmental Management to sue Rules Review Commission over veto of Phase II stormwater rules).

121. G.S. 150B-21.3(b). It is possible for a rule to become effective even later than these limits indicate, if the rule-making agency chooses a later date. *Id.*

122. G.S. 150B-21.3. In 2004 the legislature clarified that letters asking the Rules Review Commission for legislative review of a rule must be received by the RRC by the day following RRC approval of the rule. S.L. 2004-156.

123. G.S. 150B-21.3(b1).

124. G.S. 150B-21.3(c).

125. G.S. 150B-21.3(c).

126. G.S. 120-70.100 to -70.103.

127. *See* G.S. 150B-43 ("Any person who is aggrieved *by the final decision in a contested case* . . . is entitled to judicial review of the decision . . .") (*emphasis added*). "No appeal lies from an order or decision of an administrative agency of the State or from judgments of special statutory tribunals whose proceedings are not according to the course of the common law, unless the right is granted by statute." *In re* State *ex rel.* Employment Security Comm'n., 234 N.C. 651, 68 S.E.2d 311 (1951). *See also In re* Stiers, 204 N.C. 48, 167 S.E. 382 (1933) (the State cannot appeal in either civil or criminal cases except upon statutory authority); *In re* Halifax Paper Co., 259 N.C. 589, 131 S.E.2d 441 (1963).

128. For challenges to a Rules Review Commission veto of a permanent rule, see G.S. 150B-21.8(d). This provision and the statutory grant of standing to challenge temporary rules were added in 2003, so at the date of publication of this book, there has been little to no experience with them.

129. G.S. 150B-21.1(c) (temporary rules); G.S. 150B-21.1A(c) (emergency rules).

130. G.S. 150B-21.9(a1). Prior to 2003, this language was "conclusive evidence" rather than "rebuttable presumption." The legislature lowered the standard for judicial review of a permanent rule in response to requests by lobbyists for development interests, who were frustrated in their challenge to state wetland rules by the decision in *In re Ruling by Environmental Management Com'n*, 155 N.C. App. 408, 573 S.E.2d 732 (2002). It will be interesting to see whether increased litigation over rules results from the change.

131. Pue v. Hood, Comm'r of Banks, 222 N.C. 310, 22 S.E.2d 896 (1942).

132. State v. Grundler, 251 N.C. 177, 111 S.E.2d 1 (1959).

133. McDowell v. Kure Beach, 251 N.C. 818, 112 S.E.2d 390 (1960).

134. G.S. 150B-20.

135. G.S. 150B-20(b), (c).

136. G.S. 150B-21.1(c); G.S. 150B-21.1A(c).

137. *See* G.S. 150B-21.9.

138. G.S. 150B-21.1(c); G.S. 150B-21.1A(c).

139. G.S. 150B-21.15 (repealed).

140. The rule-making agency within the Department of Environment and Natural Resources was the Environmental Management Commission. The rules are now codified at 15A NCAC 2B.0101, .0103, .0202, and .0220 and 2H.0501, .0502, .0503, .0504, .0506, and .0507.

141. *In re* Ruling by Environmental Management Comm'n, 155 N.C. App. 408, 573 S.E.2d 732 (2002).

142. ATTORNEY GENERAL'S COMMITTEE ON ADMINISTRATIVE PROCEDURE, ADMINISTRATIVE PROCEDURE IN GOVERNMENT AGENCIES, S. Doc. No. 8, 77th Cong., 1st Sess., at 214–215 (1941).

143. 1939 N.C. Sess. Laws ch. 218 (providing a uniform procedure for the suspension or revocation by certain North Carolina boards and commissions of licenses to engage in trades and lawful callings). This act was codified at G.S. 150-1, *et seq.*(now repealed). Its vestiges live on as the separate Article 3A procedure for contested case hearings of certain boards, notably occupational licensing agencies.

144. Others include Massachusetts, South Carolina, Kansas, Oregon, North Dakota, South Dakota, and Wisconsin.

145. *See generally* 1 K. DAVIS, ADMINISTRATIVE LAW TREATISE §1:7, at 24 (2d ed. 1978); *see also* A. BONFIELD, STATE ADMINISTRATIVE RULE MAKING § 1.2.1, at 16–22 (1986) (BONFIELD 1986).

146. BONFIELD 1986, at 18.

147. K. DAVIS, ADMINISTRATIVE LAW TREATISE §§1.04–1.05, at 14 (1970 Supp.), reporting the twelve states to be California, Illinois, Indiana, Massachusetts, Michigan, Missouri, North Carolina, North Dakota, Ohio, Pennsylvania, Virginia, and Wisconsin.

148. G.S. 143-195 (repealed in 1973 with the passage of North Carolina's APA).

149. 1953 N.C. Sess. Laws ch. 1094 (codified as G.S. Chapter 143, Art. 33, §§ 143-306 to 143-316).

150. G.S. 143-307 (repealed), explained in *In re Halifax Paper Co.*, 259 N.C. 589 (1963).

151. ROBERT G. BYRD, *A Report to the Committee on Administrative Law of the North Carolina Bar Association on Publication of Administrative Rules and Regulations* (Chapel Hill: Institute of Government, 1960).

152. Former G.S. 143-198.1 (in addition to filing with the secretary of state, agencies created by statute and authorized to exercise regulatory, administrative, or quasi-judicial functions had to file with the clerk of superior court of each county a certified indexed copy of all rules, the violation of which would constitute a crime.)

153. BYRD at 3.

154. The original North Carolina APA, G.S. Chapter 150A, codified House Bill 1076 (ratified April 12, 1974) and was originally made effective

July 1, 1975. The effective date was delayed until February 1, 1976, by State Bill 85 (ratified March 24, 1975). The original North Carolina APA required in Article 5 that agencies file all rules, regulations, ordinances, standards, and amendments with the Attorney General's office before the rule could become effective. This excluded (1) rules, procedures, or regulations relating to internal management of the agency; (2) directives or advisory opinions to any specifically named person or group with no general applicability throughout the state; (3) dispositions of a specific issue or matter by the process of adjudication; and (4) orders establishing or fixing rates or tariffs. G.S. 150A-10 (repealed).

155. Bonfield reported twenty-eight such states: Arkansas, Connecticut, Georgia, Hawaii, Idaho, Illinois, Iowa, Louisiana, Maine, Maryland, Michigan, Mississippi, Missouri, Montana, Nebraska, Nevada, New Hampshire, New York, North Carolina, Oklahoma, Rhode Island, South Dakota, Tennessee, Vermont, Washington, West Virginia, Wisconsin, and Wyoming, as well as the District of Columbia. Bonfield notes that Prof. Davis also includes Arizona, Florida, Indiana, Massachusetts, New Mexico, and Oregon as such states. BONFIELD, 1986, at 19 n.9. Bonfield's 1993 SUPPLEMENT, citing 14 U.L.A., listed twenty-nine states, for some reason not including North Carolina. A. BONFIELD, STATE ADMINISTRATIVE RULE MAKING §1.2.2, at 3–4 (Boston: Little Brown, Supp. 1993).

156. N.C. Dep't of State Auditor, *Operational Audit: The Administrative Procedures Act* (Raleigh: March 1976).

157. *Id.* at 7.

158. BILL FINGER, JACK BETTS, RAN COBLE, AND JACK NICHOLS, ASSESSING THE ADMINISTRATIVE PROCEDURE ACT (Raleigh: N.C. Center for Public Policy Research, May 1985).

159. *Id.* at 15–19.

160. *Id.* at 24.

161. *Id* at 25.

162. *Id* at 28.

Chapter 3

How can interested persons monitor and participate in rule making?

The North Carolina Register

The *North Carolina Register* is the definitive source of information about rules in the process of being made or changed in North Carolina. Whatever other sources one consults, this is the primary and statutorily authorized publication in which notices of rule-making proceedings, the texts of proposed rules, and final actions on rules are included.[1] Subscriptions to the *North Carolina Register* are available from the Office of Administrative Hearings in Raleigh, subject to a subscription fee set by the codifier of rules in an amount to cover publication, copying, and mailing costs.[2] The publication is also widely available in libraries around the state.

The Office of Administrative Hearings Web site, http://www.oah.state.nc.us, is now the most widely available and up-to-date source of information on rules and proposed rules.

The N.C. Administrative Code (NCAC)

Just as the *North Carolina Register* is the official publication for tracking rules in the process of being made, the *North Carolina Administrative*

Code(NCAC) is the official publication that sets out what rules have been adopted. See the section in chapter 1 of this book entitled "Who collects and publishes the official version of the rules?" for more information about the *Code* and its publication.[3]

Other sources for monitoring rule making

Agency mailing lists Agencies subject to the Administrative Procedure Act (APA) rule-making provisions are required to maintain a mailing list of persons who want information about proposed rules. Agencies are allowed to charge an annual fee to people on this list, to cover copying and mailing costs.[4] For persons interested in monitoring a particular agency, the mailing list can be a useful way to track rule making.

Petition for rule making

As noted above,[5] the APA provides a way for interested persons to request an agency to adopt a rule. This procedure is rarely used, as the agencies typically have a great deal of discretion as to whether and in what form to adopt rules, but the rule-making petition is a potentially useful way for interested parties to make agencies aware of their desire for policy changes and, conceivably, to bring those policy goals before a judge.

Declaratory rulings

The APA also provides a mechanism for interested parties to use in requesting an agency to issue a declaration "as to the validity of a rule or as to the applicability to a given state of facts of a statute administered by the agency or of a rule or order of the agency."[6] This procedure, like the petition for rule making, is rarely used, in part because the statute allows an agency to duck the request "when the agency for good cause finds issuance of a ruling undesirable."[7] In fact, the agency can simply do nothing in response to a request and have that non-response treated as a denial after sixty days.[8] However, the agency is not supposed to make such a finding on an ad hoc basis; rather, it is supposed to have in its rules "the circumstances in which rulings shall or shall not be issued."[9] This type of rule, stating when the agency will or will not make a declaratory ruling, is actually rare among North Carolina agencies.

The statute for declaratory rulings, like the statute on petitions for rule making, allows a petitioner to get judicial review of the agency's action or inaction in response to the request, so this is yet another way in which interested parties can attempt to intervene in or shape the course of agency rule making.

Notes

1. Chapter 150B, Section 21.1, of the North Carolina General Statutes (hereinafter G.S.)

2. G.S. 150B-21.25.

3. See text at pages 16 to 17.

4. G.S. 150B-21.2(d).

5. See text at pages 53 to 54.

6. G.S. 150B-4.

7. G.S. 150B-4.

8. G.S. 150B-4.

9. G.S. 150B-4.

Index

About the Author

Richard B. Whisnant joined the School of Government in 1998. His areas of interest include environmental protection, natural resources management, and administrative law.

Other School of Government Publications

Cleanup Law of North Carolina: A Guide to a State's Environmental Cleanup Laws
2003
Richard B. Whisnant
Analyzes and discusses the laws that govern the cleanup of property contaminated by some form of pollution. Looks beyond statutes and appellate decisions to the actual administrative programs that put these laws in place. For people who want to know how cleanup laws really work, including owners, buyers, sellers, neighbors, and attorneys involved with property that may be contaminated.

Local Government for Environmental Policymakers
2003
Edited by Richard B. Whisnant
Provides environmental policymakers a fundamental understanding of how local governments work: how they are structured, how they are funded, what their powers are, and what drives their decision making. Readings focus on North Carolina, but the discussion can provide a more general framework and point of departure from which to understand and work with local governments in any state.

Open Meetings and Local Governments in North Carolina: Some Questions and Answers
Sixth edition, 2002
David M. Lawrence
Details the provisions of North Carolina's open meetings law in a question-and-answer format and sets out the text of the law. For a related publication, see *Local Government Law Bulletin* No. 103: "Closed Sessions under the Attorney–Client Privilege."

Guide for North Carolina State Boards, Commissions, and Councils in the Executive Branch
1999
Milton S. Heath Jr.
Offers an orientation in basic public law issues for people serving on state boards. Also serves as an introduction to the official duties and responsibilities of all citizen members of citizen boards, commissions, and councils that are policy makers and advisers to state government. Serves as a primer for prospective or new members and as a reference for more experienced members. Appendixes include constitutional provisions, selected statutes, and executive orders.

State and Local Government Relations in North Carolina: Their Evolution and Current Status
Second edition, 1995
Edited by Charles D. Liner
Examines the origins of governmental organization in North Carolina and the current allocation of responsibility for administration, finance, and policy between the state government and units of local government.

Order these and other School of Government publications online at sog.unc.edu or contact the Sales Office at sales@sog.unc.edu or 919.966.4119 to learn more about our publications program. To receive an automatic e-mail announcement when new titles are published, join the New Publications Bulletin Board Listserv by visitig sog.unc.edu/resources/microsites/listserv/listserv-list.

www.ingramcontent.com/pod-product-compliance
Lightning Source LLC
Chambersburg PA
CBHW070930270326
41927CB00011B/2801